— This book is for Sam —

Elvis Religion

THE CULT OF THE KING

— Gregory L. Reece —

I.B. TAURIS

LONDON · NEW YORK

Published in 2006 by I.B.Tauris & Co Ltd
6 Salem Road, London W2 4BU
175 Fifth Avenue, New York NY 10010
www.ibtauris.com

In the United States of America and Canada
distributed by Palgrave Macmillan a division of St Martin's Press
175 Fifth Avenue, New York NY 10010

ISBN 10: 1 84511 164 8 (Pb)
ISBN 13: 978 1 84511 164 9 (Pb)

ISBN 10: 1 84511 256 3 (Hb)
ISBN 13: 978 1 84511 256 1 (Hb)

A full CIP record for this book is available from the British Library
A full CIP record is available from the Library of Congress

Library of Congress Catalog Card Number: available

Typeset in Bookman Old Style by JCS Publishing Services
Printed and bound in Great Britain by TJ International Ltd,
Padstow, Cornwall

Contents

Acknowledgements

There are many people who helped, not only in making this book possible, but in making my Elvis journey possible. Thanks so much to Cheryl Patton for a wonderfully strange trip to Las Vegas. Thanks to Kris Daw for traveling with me to Holly Springs and turning Graceland Too into that great little film *King of Kings*. Thanks to Michael Patton for helping out at the American Academy of Religion. Thanks to Alex Wright, of I.B.Tauris for encouraging me to take this trip and for helping me along the way. Thanks to Samuel Gilbert Reece for listening as I read nearly every word of the manuscript aloud. Finally, thanks to Kristen Gilbert, my wife, for Sam and Olivia, for encouragement, for a great place to write, for making coffee, for giving me up for so long, for keeping the kids quiet, for reading the manuscript, for everything.

Introduction

My first real encounter with Elvis occurred in 1991, appropriately enough on a sweltering summer night in Memphis, Tennessee. Like many people, I knew who Elvis was and was aware of at least some of his hit songs and a little of his life story. Elvis's music had mostly played in the background of my life. I heard it on movie soundtracks, or blaring from a broken speaker on a jukebox. I never listened carefully. It was the same with the story of his life. I knew what everybody in the American south knew about Elvis Presley but not much else. He started out in poverty, then, on the strength of his talent, his personality, his good looks, and his will, he rose far beyond his upbringing. In doing so he invented rock and roll, made young girls faint, and swiveled his hips on the *Ed Sullivan Show*. Throughout his life he remained true to his family and his faith. He was a devoted Christian, gave Cadillacs away by the dozen, and was always true to his word. Tragically, however, the bright lights had gotten the best of this simple country boy from Mississippi. The constant demands and harrowing schedule had taken their toll. Elvis had become addicted to drugs and died of an overdose.

The story of Elvis that I knew was a story without details but filled with moral lessons. It told, first, a lesson about working hard and using whatever talent you had to better yourself. Even a boy raised in poverty in Mississippi (or in my case, Alabama) could make it big. But, it was also a cautionary tale where the moral could be taken in quite another way. Success and fame may look good on the surface but they can be dangerous. Elvis would have been better off and happier if he had just stayed in Tupelo. It was a story, in its two contrasting moral elements, that served as something of an excuse for southern white people. Oh, we could make it big, we could be rich and famous, just look at Elvis, but we choose not to follow this path. The simple life is a happier life, just look at Elvis. I knew the broad strokes of this narrative and took the lessons to heart, but in no way saw them as significant or important.

In the summer of 1991 I found myself in the waiting area of a hospital emergency room in Memphis, Tennessee, well after midnight. I noticed as I took my seat that the woman sitting next to me had been crying. She must have been in her late fifties and wore her grey hair in a style that had no doubt been popular in her teenage years. Her face was heavily made up and, because of her tears, was in great disarray. As soon as I had settled into the chair, magazine in hand, she started to tell me her story.

Her mother had suffered a stroke and she was waiting to hear from the doctors. This was especially difficult, she said, because she had no other family in Memphis. A few years before, she had divorced her husband, said goodbye to her children, packed up her mother, and moved from southern California to Memphis, Tennessee. She moved, she said, 'just to be with Elvis.' It was then that I noticed that the ring on her left hand, as well as her earrings and necklace, were adorned with images of Elvis. Elvis, she told me, was the most important thing in the world to her. He gave her inspiration and hope. The one good thing about the inevitable passing away of her mother was that her mother would then get to go to heaven to be with Elvis.

I did not get the woman's name. I do not know how things turned out with her mother. The dynamics of a hospital emergency room shifted her attention, or mine, to something else and the story was never completed. I realized, however, following this encounter, that there might be more to Elvis than I knew, that he might be far more important to some people than he was to me. To me, he was an element in my cultural background. This woman, however, spoke of him in terms reminiscent of religious devotion. Elvis gave her inspiration and hope. Her loved ones would go to be with him when they died. From that night on, though I would never be devoted to Elvis, I would be interested in Elvis devotion, interested in the way the figure of Elvis Presley has come to be shrouded in religious imagery, not just for lonely hearts late at night in Memphis emergency rooms, or for Elvis impersonators on a Las Vegas stage, but in such mainstream venues as Hollywood movies, fiction, popular music, and art. Elvis, saint and savior, I would discover, is everywhere.

The trajectory of this book in many ways follows the trajectory of my own quest to understand the religious phenomena associated with Elvis. As my encounter with Saint Elvis began in Memphis, Tennessee, so Memphis is the place to begin looking for Elvis devotion. Other writers have seen in Memphis the beginnings of a cult of Elvis. Elvis's Memphis home, Graceland, has been described as a religious shrine and as the focus of annual pilgrimages by the faithful. Chapter 1 is an examination of the idea of Graceland as a religious shrine and an account of my own experiences in Memphis during happy hour at the Heartbreak Hotel. Chapter 2 offers a look at another element of Elvis fandom that is often treated as a religious phenomenon: Elvis impersonators. This chapter will examine the phenomenon of Elvis tribute artists and relate my personal tale of a very strange Halloween weekend in Las Vegas.

The next phase of this book expands the search for Saint Elvis beyond the circle of Elvis fans and impersonators and examines religious images of Elvis found in mainstream popular culture and as developed by filmmakers, authors, and song writers. Chapter 3 offers a look at Hollywood's contributions to the Elvis mythos. Chapter

4 examines religious themes associated with Elvis in fiction. Chapter 5 considers the presence of Saint Elvis in popular music.

Finally, this book explores the presence of Saint Elvis in aspects of culture that are neither mainstream nor closely associated with the traditional Elvis communities of fans and impersonators. Chapter 6 is a look at the occurrence of religious images of Elvis in outsider art, and includes an account of my personal experiences with Paul MacLeod's Graceland Too. The religious presence of Elvis on the internet is the subject of Chapter 7. Chapter 8, the final point in our journey, explores the sometimes bizarre world of Elvis's tabloid presence, including Elvis sightings and Elvis conspiracy theories.

It is hoped that this book will offer much that will be of help in understanding Elvis and religion, and do so without going over too much ground that has been covered before. While there are books that examine Elvis's influence upon popular culture in a more general sense, and books that explore the phenomena of Elvis fans and impersonators with an eye toward their religious significance, I do not believe that there has yet been an investigation of Elvis and religion that goes beyond these rather small communities to include an appraisal of the religious significance of Elvis Presley for popular culture more broadly conceived. This is the task that I pursue here. The benefits of this approach are pretty important, I believe. First of all, by looking beyond the insular communities of Elvis fans and impersonators we are able to see that religious interpretations of Elvis Presley constitute more than a fringe group phenomenon. They are, in contrast, becoming an accepted part of the popular culture landscape. Second, the approach taken by this book allows for the inclusion of a critical feature of the religious phenomena of Elvis Presley that is often overlooked by a more limited focus upon the most dedicated devotees: the important role played by irony in many man-ifestations of Elvis devotion.

Before officially getting underway with this examination of Elvis and religion, I must begin by mentioning an element of my experience that, though not quite fitting into the main argument of the book, is nevertheless important for an understanding of the topic at hand. I am referring to the fact that no matter where I have traveled or in what context I have found myself, there have always been people who wanted to tell me their personal story about Elvis. As a mat-ter of fact, one of the joys of researching this book has been watching the response of people when I have told them the nature of this project. Many of them have then immediately volunteered a story of their own, most of which did not find a way into this text, but all of which helped to make me understand a little more about the magnitude of the impact of Elvis Presley upon our culture.

There was, for example, the man in his thirties who reminisced about the day that Elvis died and how his family had played one Elvis record after another for nearly a week following the tragic news. He could not say that anyone in his family had really been an Elvis fan, and he had never really listened to his music since, but it had, nevertheless, become burned into his memory as one of the most impor-tant events in his childhood. Or, take the story of the elderly gentleman who, speaking up quietly and without any fanfare, confessed that he had been in the New York audience – on the front row, no less – for Elvis's appearance on the *Ed Sullivan Show*. 'What did you think?' I asked him. 'I thought he did a fine job,' he replied.

And then there is my own story, for I grew up in the deep south, a child of ten when the news of Elvis's death came over the radio. What I remember most about that day, a hot August day when it was better to stay indoors and avoid the ravenous humidity, what I remember most is running the half mile to my cousin Theresa's house, oblivious to the heat. Theresa, you see, was in my estimation at the time the biggest Elvis fan in the world. A couple of years older than me and now allowed to decorate her room to her own taste, her bedroom walls were covered with posters of Elvis. I remember knowing that I needed to find Theresa, not so that I could comfort her, for my ten-year-old self was barely capable of thinking first of how to help someone else, but to have her tell me why this news was so important, why everyone at home was talking about it, and how I myself should respond. I am too young to remember the assassination of JFK or MLK, too young to remember the moon landing or Watergate. My first national memory, my first memory of a world-significant event, is my memory of the death of Elvis.

1

Elvis in Memphis
Happy Hour at the Heartbreak Hotel

The parking lot of 'Elvis Presley's Heartbreak Hotel' was filled with cars sporting personalized Elvis license plates. Variations on 'TCB' were the most common, in tribute to Elvis's personal logo consisting of these three letters and a lightning bolt. Elvis, it seems, believed in 'Taking Care of Business' in a flash. There were also hound dogs, (HNDDG and other variations), KINGs, and EAPs (Elvis Aron Presley). My own, non-Elvis and non-personalized plate stood out like a sore thumb. Obviously I was going to be among Elvis fans. This was not exactly surprising to me. After all, the next day was Elvis's birthday and I was in Memphis, Tennessee, just across the street from Elvis's Graceland mansion. It was a little before eight o'clock and the frigid wind made me glad that I was on my way to the hotel bar rather than to a candlelight vigil at Graceland's Meditation Garden. This, I thought, as I entered the door of the lobby, is as good as it gets for Elvis fans. It's Elvis's birthday eve and happy hour at the Heartbreak Hotel.

After grabbing a drink from the bar, and a bag of complimentary popcorn, I found a seat at the end of one of many large tables that crowded the room. The room, I quickly decided based on the presence of a cereal bar shoved against the far wall, must, under normal conditions, serve as the location of the hotel's continental breakfast. This night, however, it was so much more than that. The lights were low, a good-looking and fit young Elvis impersonator was performing, and the crowd, probably seventy-five or so, mostly middle-aged women, seemed to be loving it. Many members of the audience knew the performer's routine and had come prepared to participate. For example, when the performer began singing Elvis's 'Devil in Disguise', all of the women at my table jumped up and ran to the front of the room to join him. They then proceeded to dance around wildly, adorned with flashing red devil horns atop their heads. After the song they came back to the table breathless and laughing hysterically. Likewise, a little later in the show, as the performer broke into 'Viva Las Vegas', two very slender young women hopped up to dance with him, ripping off their skirts to reveal white short-shorts like those I had seen Ann-Margret wear in the movie of the same name. They, too, returned to their seats in a spasm of laughter.

During the intermission the talk at my table was about the wedding that was to take place at Graceland the next day. This conversation had been sparked by the arrival of the groom a bit earlier in the evening, delivering a rose to his bride. The bride, apparently, was spending the night before her wedding along with other Elvis fans in the hotel bar. There was no word as to what the groom would be doing. The gossip from the women at my table was that the bride and groom were fan club presidents from different parts of England who had become acquainted some years before at an Elvis birthday gathering at Graceland. The previous year he had popped the big question on the front steps of the mansion. She said 'yes' to the proposal and the administration of Graceland said 'yes' to hosting the wedding. It was, everyone seemed to agree, a match made in heaven.

Just as intermission was coming to an end, everyone's attention turned to a new arrival in the room, a child of eight or nine dressed in an Elvis jumpsuit with sunglasses and jet-black hair. The crowd, consisting, I supposed, mostly of grandmothers, could not get enough of the young Elvis, who oddly looked more like the older Elvis. Everyone wanted to snap his picture, for which he would pose, without a smile, but with the requisite snarl.

And the evening went on. There were more songs from the impersonator, some of them accompanied by the placing of scarves around the necks and the kissing of the cheeks of the most enthusiastic women in the audience. Audience members were invited to shout out their place of origin. (Australia! Texas! England! France! Ohio!) When the show was over, the crowd seemed happy just to stay where they were. Some, of course, left with the music, but some stayed around to talk. Many of them made a point of speaking to, or even hugging, the bride to-be. Everybody seemed relaxed and hesitant to leave. It stuck me that the people seemed, above all else, comfortable, as if they were among friends. I felt the same way, after all the beer was cold and the popcorn was free. Happy Birthday, Elvis!

— Elvis Presley's Graceland —

Elvis Presley Boulevard in Memphis, Tennessee, is a busy four-lane highway lined with old strip malls, used-car lots, and pawn shops. It is evident that at one time, maybe in the 1950s and 1960s, it was a prosperous part of town. Far away from downtown Memphis, it must have been a nice suburban community. Nestled, as one might have called it then, between the Memphis Airport and the Mississippi state line it would have been a bridge community, linking urban Memphis with the bucolic, rural communities of north Mississippi. Its name, before it later became a part of the city of Memphis, was Whitehaven, and indeed it was a place popular with white families in their flight from black

Memphis. As it is, however, urban and black Memphis has, quite ironically, come to Whitehaven and Elvis Presley Boulevard, and white families have gone east to Collierville and further south to the optimistically named Olive Branch, Mississippi.

It was here, in this community, that Elvis bought an estate containing a modest mansion. When Elvis moved in the estate was already called Graceland, after the daughter of its Civil War era owner, but the name would become synonymous with Elvis, even more so after his death than during his life. And so, people from all over the world who might otherwise never dream of visiting Memphis, Tennessee, or if they did would never dream of leaving the downtown riverfront with the Peabody Hotel's trained ducks and Beale Street's blues and booze, come to Elvis Presley Boulevard. They come to Graceland, the home and final resting place of the King of Rock and Roll.

Across the street, that is, across the busy four-lane highway, from the Graceland Mansion stands Graceland Plaza, a strip mall-like complex that blends in pretty well with the strip malls up and down Elvis Presley Boulevard. Graceland Plaza includes gift shops filled with Elvis-themed merchandise, my favorite being a salt-and-pepper shaker set in the shape of a lunchbox and thermos with Elvis's image and the words 'All Shook Up' emblazoned on the side. I suppose it is intended as a crossover item, with appeal to Elvis fans, salt-and-pepper set aficionados, and lunchbox collectors. In addition to the gift shops, Graceland Plaza includes a theater that shows a documentary about Elvis's life, museums focusing on items from Elvis's personal life and his automobile collection, themed restaurants, and two airplanes which are open for tours – *The Lisa Marie* and *The Hound Dog II*.

For the most part Graceland Plaza provides a place for tourists to be entertained, and spend money, while waiting for the tour of Graceland itself. Visitors are bused across

Elvis Presley Boulevard and up the drive of Graceland in order to take a tour of the mansion. The tour allows visitors to see some of the ground-floor rooms from behind a velvet rope, including the living room, music room, dining room, kitchen, television room (with three wall-mounted televisions – the height of technological luxury in the 1970s, one supposes), pool room, and the 'jungle room,' so named for its African-themed décor. In addition, tourists are taken to an adjacent building to see Vernon Presley's office and another museum that includes Elvis's gold records and a small collection of his jumpsuits. Finally, tourists are allowed to visit the Meditation Garden to view the graves of Elvis and his immediate family. After that, it is back on the bus for the ride across Elvis Presley Boulevard and the return to Graceland Plaza. After tour hours are officially over the gates are kept open for a couple of hours and visitors are allowed to walk up the drive to the Meditation Garden.

Those who choose to walk along the sidewalk in front of Graceland will find a stone wall that has become a focal point for those wishing to leave their mark or to leave a message for Elvis. The wall is covered with graffiti left by fans and visitors. Though the Graceland staff clean the wall regularly, tourists quickly fill up all available space again. Daniel Wright, in his book *Dear Elvis: Graffiti from Graceland*, has preserved a snapshot of this graffiti for posterity. Most are simply the sort of silly impromptu comments a tourist to Graceland might be expected to leave:

Elvis = Cute! (Wright 1996: 21)

Some, however, verge on the philosophical:

In the great divide between a life with meaning and one without, there is Graceland. (30)

Others refer to the fact that Elvis is still alive:

> Elvis is alive and works security at Northside Mall in Slidell, LA. (42)

Some are remarkably personal:

> Elvis, yesterday I realized how much I love you, so I broke off my engagement to Adam. Please come home to Mama! – Monique. (18)

Others are just plain weird:

> E, thanks for carpeting the ceilings of our hearts! (17)

And some seem downright religious:

> As long as we keep Elvis on our minds there is a promised land for the future. (45)

The busiest time of the year at Graceland is the week surrounding the anniversary of Elvis's death in August. A smaller version of these festivities takes place in January, in celebration of Elvis's birthday. The August festivities include an Elvis impersonator contest, a hotel room window decoration contest, fan club meetings, and a candlelight vigil and procession to the Meditation Garden, which is adorned with floral arrangements and teddy bears presented by fan clubs from across the country and around the world. The silent vigil is a solemn occasion marked by tears, prayers, and quiet reflection. It is no doubt the central element of the Graceland experience for many devoted fans. In *E: Reflections on the Birth of the Elvis Faith*, John Strausbaugh estimates the crowd at between ten and twenty thousand people in the year of his attendance (1995: 60). Erika Doss reports the attendance in 1997, the twentieth anniversary of Elvis's death, as sixty thousand (1999: 91). Actual figures are hard to determine, especially considering the fact that many fans make the round trip up and down the drive multiple times throughout the night, but I am extremely skeptical that it would be logistically possible for sixty thousand people to descend upon Graceland, Graceland Plaza, and Elvis Presley Boulevard without ushering in the apocalypse. It seems to me that there simply are not enough hotels, parking places, or routes in and out to make this possible. In any event, a lot of people turn out for the celebration of Elvis's birth and the remembrance of his death.

— Pilgrims and Shrines —

The phenomena associated with Graceland, especially those surrounding the candlelight vigil, have led some to make rather direct comparisons between Elvis fans and religious pilgrims. One of the earliest and most influential proponents of such a view is Ted Harrison, whose book *Elvis People: The Cult of the King* advances the claims that the phenomena associated with Elvis fans resemble those associated with a cult, and this Elvis cult may one day become a full-fledged religion (1992: 9). The aspects of the Elvis cult as identified by Harrison are several, and are probably familiar to many readers, considering that they have been the focus of both serious journalism and scholarship as well as of media sensationalism and outright parody.

First, Elvis is referred to as the 'King,' a term with clear religious connotations within the Christian faith where Jesus himself is referred to as the 'King of Kings.' Second, fans recount Elvis's life story in much the way that early Christians told the story of Jesus and wrote gospels. This retelling of the life story of Elvis includes tales of his good deeds, often associated with the giving away of Cadillacs and his kindness toward his mother, as well as stories of his own religious faith and devotion. Third, Elvis fans attribute a sacred character to certain objects associated with Elvis, thus granting them the status of relics and icons. Fans collect Elvis souvenirs, often purchased at Graceland Plaza, and in extreme cases even collect items from Elvis's personal life such as toenails and his used water cups. Fourth, Elvis impersonators constitute a form of priesthood for Elvis fans. Dressed in the vestments of the religion, they mediate between fans and the spirit of the King, incarnating Elvis through their reenactment of his performances. Fifth, Elvis fans participate in charitable activities in Elvis's name. These often focus on Memphis area hospitals. Sixth, Elvis is said to be alive, even after his death – in some cases by those who would attribute this life to a spiritual presence and in other cases by people who actually claim to have seen Elvis physically alive. This claim presents an interesting parallel to the disagreement between the early followers of Jesus as to whether his resurrection was physical or purely spiritual. Seventh, Elvis fans make pilgrimages to Elvis shrines, namely his birthplace in Tupelo, Mississippi, and Graceland in Memphis, Tennessee. The Graceland shrine is of particular importance as it is the place of his burial and the scene of the central liturgy of the Elvis cult, the candlelight vigil.

Other authors have followed Harrison and made very similar claims about Elvis fans. John Strausbaugh suggests that Elvis fans are creating another indigenous American religion, like Black Islam or Mormonism (1995: 10). He identifies several facets of Elvis devotion that seem to support this claim. While many of Strausbaugh's claims are simply restatements of Harrison's observations concerning the social behavior of Elvis devotees, Strausbaugh is also interested in the content of the beliefs concerning Elvis held by fans and followers. According to Strausbaugh, Elvis devotees believe that:

1   Elvis is a mythic King who has left the presence of his
    people but is not really dead.

2 Elvis is a supernatural being who watches over them from above and may intervene on their behalf.
3 The nature of Elvis has been revealed through miraculous cures and visions.
4 Elvis will return to earth or be reunited with his followers in heaven. (Strausbaugh 1995: 11–12)

For both Harrison and Strausbaugh, Graceland stands as the central point of the Elvis cult. It is the *axis mundi* of the Elvis universe. It is the place where Elvis lived, the place where Elvis died, and the place where Elvis is buried. It is a gathering point for Elvis fans from around the world, and the location of the most moving of all tributes to Elvis. Elvis researcher Erika Doss agrees with this appraisal of the centrality of Graceland in the development of an Elvis religion. She also, however, reveals one of the most crucial problems associated with this understanding of the phenomena. Namely, most Elvis fans, most people who visit Graceland, even most people who participate in the candlelight vigil, would not be comfortable in describing Graceland as a religious shrine.

> Religious terms like 'pilgrimage' and 'shrine' are generally not part of the average Graceland visitor's vocabulary, and many fans might be offended if they heard these words used in relation to their visits to the site. Still, Elvis's estate has become the object of veneration for thousands of fans who visit it every year, and for thousands more who wish that they, too, could go to Graceland. (Doss 1999: 85–86)

In other words, Doss recognizes that in interpreting Graceland as a shrine or sacred space she is offering an interpretation that most fans and visitors to Graceland would reject. Yet, oddly enough, she insists on the aptness of the interpretation, nevertheless. This is a problem that she recognizes time and time again. For example, she claims that fans engage in specific rituals during Elvis weeks, but notes that most fans would fail to see these activities as rituals (91). What, we may ask, are these rituals that fans participate in, apparently in ignorance? What are these cultic observances that are at the heart of Elvis faith? Doss offers a list, more detailed than that given by Harrison or Strausbaugh, and because it is more detailed, also more telling. We are told that Elvis fans

1 take the Graceland tour,
2 attend fan club meetings and collectors auctions,
3 engage in charity work,
4 attend benefit concerts for local hospitals,
5 donate blood to the Elvis Presley Trauma Center,
6 attend lectures and memorial services,
7 attend impersonator contests,
8 visit local landmarks associated with Elvis,
9 write on the Graceland wall,
10 drink iced tea at the Graceland Plaza restaurant, and
11 eat at the Shoney's fried chicken buffet down the street from Graceland (Doss 1999: 91–92).

This, it seems to me, is a very odd list. If one is trying to demonstrate, against the protest of participants, that the events surrounding the observance of Elvis's birth and death constitute some sort of religious rituals, this list of what Elvis fans actually do in Memphis does not strike me as all that convincing. Doss's list sounds more like the kind of things that one does at academic conferences or at business or hobbyist conventions. If these activities constitute religious rituals, then so do the convention activities of accountants, comic-book collectors, academics, and booksellers. Yes, it is true, visitors to Graceland, especially the diehard fans who come in August and in January, participate in very similar events year after year. In that very loose sense of the word I suppose that we could say that they, therefore, participate in rituals. It seems to me, however, that we have now loosened our definition of ritual to the point where it no longer serves as an indicator of religious phenomena. By these standards almost all human behavior is ritualistic behavior. Consequently, I remain unconvinced that the religious hypothesis is borne out and that a new cult or religion is in its infancy at Graceland.

— Happy Birthday, Elvis —

Following a scavenger hunt at Graceland open to the presidents of officially recognized Elvis Presley fan clubs (journalists and researchers not invited) and a day of meetings by Elvis fan clubs and collectors' societies, shopping at Graceland Plaza, and tours of Graceland, many of the participants at Elvis's birthday celebration ended his birthday in the same way they had ended the day before: by gathering for beer and popcorn at the Heartbreak Hotel bar. After sticking my head in the door long enough to ascertain that the crowd and the festivities looked an awful lot like what I had seen the night before, I headed out to Elvis Presley Boulevard and dropped in on another Elvis-themed bar located in a nearby strip mall.

The atmosphere here was remarkably like that at the hotel, though perhaps a bit less reminiscent of a continental-breakfast bar. An Elvis impersonator was on stage, a little older than the one I had seen the night before, but fit and trim and in command of the music. He seemed to know almost everyone in the place, stopping between songs to call them by name and reminisce about Elvis birthday parties past. He also told a lot of stories about his own near brushes with Elvis and his acquaintance with people who actually knew and worked for the King. He had, we were told, recently been given a cigarette lighter that had once belonged to Elvis. It seems that Elvis had enjoyed smoking cigars and was always asking his bodyguards for a match. One Christmas they had chipped in together to buy him a monogrammed cigarette lighter. Elvis was so touched by the thoughtfulness of the gift that he refused to carry the lighter, in fear that he would lose it, and had put it away unused.

At one table in the center of the room was a group comprised of women in their late thirties or early forties. The group stood out because each of the women had their hair dyed and styled in a fashion reminiscent of the 1950s or 1960s. They sported, without exception, either jet-black hair like Priscilla Presley on her wedding day, or platinum-blonde hair, like Marilyn Monroe. They seemed to be accompanied by husbands who had made no effort to match the style of their wives. The waitress was kind enough to tell me that the women were members of a fan club and liked to dress the part for their annual meeting in Memphis. Apparently, the rest of the year, they style their hair in more contemporary fashion.

Here, unlike the hotel bar, drink service was provided to the tables, and the luxury of having beer delivered seemed to make people drink a little more. The talk, during the intermission, was lively and mostly about the weekend's events. People wanted to tell their friends how they had managed to trade this particular picture of Elvis for that particular 45 rpm record. They wanted to tell their friends how they had finally met in person the individual they had been chatting with online for so long. They told about how much money their clubs had raised this year for charity. They told about their grandkids, bringing out pictures from their purses. They swapped stories about their health, or about the health of old friends who couldn't make it this year. They exchanged phone numbers and email addresses. They laughed, and drank, and talked, and laughed some more. Oh, and they sang, all together, 'Happy Birthday' to Elvis. On that number, and perhaps a few others, I found myself joining in.

— Conclusion —

Is Graceland a center of a new religious movement? Is it a sacred shrine at the center of a religious pilgrimage? Or is it simply the logical meeting place for Elvis fan clubs, Elvis collectors, and Elvis impersonators? Is the title 'King' more like the title of 'Lord' bestowed by believers upon Jesus or Krishna, or more like the title of 'Chairman of the Board' bestowed upon Frank Sinatra, or 'The Boss' given to Bruce Springsteen? Do Elvis memorabilia constitute religious relics and icons or are they just collectables, like Beanie Babies or old Avon bottles? What makes the charitable activities of Elvis fan clubs religious in a way that the charitable activities of other organizations are not? Do devotees make a pilgrimage to the shrine of Graceland, or do fans, collectors, and hobbyists meet there for conventions and social gatherings?

I have to say that I remain unconvinced that the Graceland phenomena share enough qualities with recognized genuine religious activities to warrant the conclusion that Memphis is the center of a developing 'cult of the King' or that one can observe there the 'birth of the Elvis Faith.' Despite my long ago, late-night encounter with a genuine Elvis devotee in a Memphis emergency room, my subsequent visits to Memphis and Graceland revealed not so much a religious movement centered around the shrine of Graceland and the person of Elvis Presley as the activities of a group of fun-loving people who associate together once or twice a year to share their interest in Elvis. They are collectors of Elvis memorabilia and artifacts. They are members of Elvis fan clubs. Is their behavior a little out of the mainstream? You bet it is. I mean, come on, they style their hair in the fashion of 1956 and dress in white, rhinestone-studded jumpsuits. They collect Elvis lunchboxes, and Elvis salt-and-pepper shaker sets, and Elvis salt-and-pepper shaker sets in the shape of lunchboxes (and now, I should say, so do I). They drive cars with personalized Elvis license plates, wear enormous costume jewelry patterned after that worn by a dead rock star, and know the words to even the most obscure Elvis Presley songs. They even love Elvis's movies. Yes, all of this is a little strange. Yes, all of this is, by many people's standards, a little bit in bad taste. But, and now I know I'm going to make enemies, it is not really any stranger than people who collect comic books, dress like superheroes at annual conventions, and know every issue of *The Amazing Spider Man* produced by Stan Lee and Steve Ditko. Elvis fans are not all that different from people who obsess over a particular breed of dog, a particular mint of coin, a particular make of car, a particular political candidate, or a particular sports team. These activities may seem strange to those who are not so inclined, they may border on obsessions, they may even descend into bad taste – but none of these facts is reason enough to identify the activities as religious.

Of course, it does happen to be the case that Elvis fans and collectors do have an obvious place to gather, in a way that many other groups do not. By opening Elvis's home to tours, the Presley estate made sure of that. They also have logical occasions on which to meet together, the anniversaries of Elvis's birth and his death. Furthermore, in the annual candlelight vigil, Elvis fans do participate in an activity centered at Graceland that does have many of the markings of a religious observance. However, services of remembrance are a common response to events that are perceived as great tragedies and losses, or, for that matter, in honor of great and significant events or important and influential people. Martin Luther King, Jr. has been granted an official state holiday in the USA and, considering the number of local and national ceremonies that mark this occasion, more people participate in rituals on this day than participate in the annual Graceland candlelight vigil. Furthermore, they do so in ceremonies that frequently include prayers and hymns. Are many of these religious ceremonies? Yes. Do they constitute the emergence of a new religious movement centered on the work of the slain civil-rights leader? No. Likewise with the candlelight vigil, there are religious elements in the ceremony, but this fact does not serve as evidence that a new cult is being born, but rather that people see fit to respond to the life and death of Elvis Presley in ways that rely on the resources of their religious beliefs.

I went to Graceland looking for religion. I went looking for pilgrims and worshippers. I went looking for people in prayer and meditation, for people bowing before shrines and icons, and making offerings to Saint Elvis. I did not find what I was looking for, but what I did find did not disappoint me. I found fans. I found collectors. I found a group of people who share common interests and who like to get together to have fun. I found a gathering of individuals from all over the world who share a common interest and like to get together regularly to share stories, and collectables, and popcorn, and beer. I found happy hour at the Heartbreak Hotel.

2

Elvis Incarnate:

Impersonators, Tribute Artists, and Priests

Paul MacLeod, proprietor of Graceland Too and self-proclaimed 'World's Greatest Elvis Fan,' gives a tour of his Elvis-themed museum that moves at breakneck speed, a necessary condition for completing the tour in under two hours. He barely stops to catch his breath as he leads visitors from one dimly lit room of Elvis paraphernalia to another. An experienced visitor to Graceland Too, however, may be able to get in a few questions if they are timed just right. I managed to get an answer to a question on one of my tours of Graceland Too by shouting it over the heads of other guests as Paul was about to take us from one room of his antebellum museum to another. 'How old are you Paul?' I called out. Paul paused, smiled, and then replied 'Sixty-four. But when I dye my hair and put on my suit, twenty-one.' I suspect that Paul is speaking for a lot of Elvis impersonators when he says that dressing like Elvis makes him feel young, vibrant, and sexy, that it is somehow transformative and life affirming. This may not be the only reason why Elvis is impersonated to a greater extent than any other celebrity, dead or alive, or why the image of the 'Elvis Impersonator' is a common image in fiction and film, but it certainly must be one of the reasons. After all, if Elvis could continue to be full of energy and sexuality after he had put on a few pounds and grown a little older, perhaps the rest of us can too. Dressing like Elvis, from the bell-bottomed jumpsuit with rhinestones and cape, to the big sunglasses and mutton chops, might just work. After all, in what other context do working-class men get to dress up, do their hair, put on makeup, adorn themselves with jewelry, and still present an image that is fully heterosexual and masculine?

What this psycho-sexual explanation overlooks, however, is that the origins of Elvis impersonation can be most clearly found in the very different careers of Andy Kaufman and Jimmy Ellis – known professionally as Orion – both of whom were driven by motives far more complex than the psycho-sexual one. While Elvis impersonations had cropped up here and there in Elvis's lifetime, they were most often either one-time performances or part of more general celebrity impersonation acts. Andy Kaufman, with his dead-on impersonation of Elvis on *Saturday Night Live*, helped to change that, however. Kaufman's act presented Elvis as the alter ego of his 'Latka' personality, a quiet unassuming immigrant who unleashes the Elvis within and by doing so becomes transformed from the shy immigrant to someone who is both sexually charged and fully American. Elvis, the rumors said, loved Kaufman's performance.

That performance, while unleashing elements of sexuality and patriotism, nevertheless was at its heart a joke, part of Kaufman's ironic take on American life that would lead, at its most bizarre, to wrestling matches with women. Consequently, while the sexual elements of Elvis impersonation cannot be overlooked, neither can its ironic elements. Kaufman's performances helped to instigate the first wave of Elvis impersonations and they have left an indelible mark on the phenomenon. There is a blurred line that separates sincerity and irony in the performance of most Elvis impersonators, in the reaction of the audiences that gather to watch and participate, and in the reception given to them by the larger culture.

Financial gain and the quest for fame also play an important role in the Elvis impersonator phenomenon. The career of Orion, one of the original and most well-known impersonators, was clearly driven by financial considerations, if not for Orion/Ellis himself, at least for his backers. Jimmy Ellis, a native of Alabama, first recorded for Sun Studios as early as 1972, when he produced covers of some of Presley's earlier hits. These records were distinctive because Ellis's singing voice sounded so much like that of Elvis. In 1978, Ellis caused a bit of a stir when his voice was added to a previously recorded single by Jerry Lee Lewis from Sun Records and he was credited on the record only as 'a friend.' The financial incentive for keeping Ellis's identity a secret was obvious. Speculation swirled around the single as people assumed this to be a previously unreleased single by Elvis himself, now deceased. When ABC Television had the recording analyzed and announced that it was indeed the voice of Elvis, the illusion seemed complete.

There was more money to be made from Ellis's striking vocal similarity to Elvis, however, and Sun Records' Shelby Singleton decided to pursue the illusion by linking Ellis with a fictional character created by Gail Brewer-Giorgio in her book *Orion*, about a rock star who fakes his own death to escape the trials of fame. Ellis was made to look like Elvis, with sideburns and jumpsuits. His face was covered with a Lone Ranger-style mask, and he was introduced to the world as 'Orion.' His first album, *Reborn* was illustrated by an image of an empty casket. The message was clear. Orion was Elvis Presley reborn. While Orion never became a major recording artist, and while he certainly never reached the level of fame of Elvis himself, he did illustrate that evoking the image of Elvis could sell records and make money.

Simple explanations, however, are bound to be too simple, and those advanced here are probably no exception. For example, they do not fully take into account the deep sense of devotion that many impersonators feel for the King of Rock 'n' Roll. Likewise ignored is the genuine sense of camaraderie and friendship that has developed within the tribute artist community; a community that, judging by the diversity of its membership in terms of ethnicity, race, and talent, is extremely accepting and open. Furthermore, these simple explanations do not come to terms with the fact that the Elvis impersonator is sometimes said to take on the characteristics of a priest or minister.

John Strausbaugh offers just such an interpretation of Elvis impersonators. They are the King's ministers, a royal priesthood that is able, through ritual and vestments, to incarnate the living presence of Elvis himself. Strausbaugh describes the phenomenon in this way:

> I've . . . witnessed Elvis reaching out and touching one of his anointed . . . translating him from an ordinary shlump into the King's messenger on earth. I've felt the King's presence electrify a room, transforming it into something like Eliade's sacred space, an ecstatic zone outside of normal space and time.
>
> If the Elvis faith develops into a full fledged religion, the Elvii are there to become its priesthood. They've got the vestments, the liturgy, the ritual, and the faithful congregation. (Strausbaugh 1995: 151–152)

Likewise, Ted Harrison presents a similar religious interpretation of Elvis impersonation.

> Can it be argued that the Elvis cult has a priesthood? Yes, though it is not a formal priesthood with established practices of apprenticeship, training, and initiation. But that is only because the cult is so new. The priesthood exists as a body of men, or at least almost exclusively men, who dress in a style of clothing

which can be compared to vestments. They perform certain actions to bring the devotees closer to the one they adore, to be a perpetual memory of the man from whom they are separated and in their own bodies they represent that man and the memory to the people when they gather for that purpose. (Harrison 1992: 101)

Are these interpreters onto something? Is it possible that the impersonator phenomenon is best understood, not as a psycho-sexual, ironic, or capitalist phenomenon, but as a religious one? My journeys to Graceland failed to reveal the presence of a religious cult devoted to Elvis Presley, but is it possible that Elvis impersonators, in many ways a group of people far more devoted to Elvis than the average Graceland visitor (I mean, come on, they dress like Elvis!) might themselves constitute an Elvis priesthood, transmitting the gospel of Elvis to the world? Are the men in white jumpsuits, capes, and sunglasses somehow equivalent to the apostles of Jesus, themselves forming the genesis of a new religious community? I had only one choice, I had to go to Las Vegas!

— Impersonators and Tribute Artists —

Elvis Expo 2004

My first real-life encounter with Elvis impersonators took place, appropriately enough, in Las Vegas, the city that is, after Memphis, Tennessee, most associated with Elvis Presley. In the past my visits to Las Vegas had always been limited to the high-rise, luxury casinos on the famous Strip, or the old style, glitter gulch casinos on Fremont Street. Elvis Expo 2004, billed as an 'All-Star Show, Convention, and Tribute Artist World Championship,' however, took place out of town on Boulder Highway in an area that was, I was told, the favorite gambling location for Las Vegas locals. The fact that the event was taking place in a decidedly less high-dollar district than I was accustomed to, combined with my stereotypical understanding of impersonators as being a little strange (not to mention the fact that tickets to the event cost $150) left me a little uncertain as to whether or not coming to Elvis Expo 2004 was such a good idea. My misgivings were only reinforced when I dropped by the convention room to take a look at some of the promised vendors only to find, for the most part, individuals who seemed to be selling items from their personal collections of Elvis memorabilia, old souvenir Elvis mugs and copies of *TV Guide* magazines featuring Elvis on the cover.

My misgivings, however, quickly turned out to be misplaced. Once the Tribute Artist World Championship got under way I ended up having one of the best times I have ever had in Sin City. What I discovered was that most of the people in attendance for the event were either tribute artists or the family and (very) close friends of tribute artists, a fact that, considering the price of admission and registration fees for contestants, was not all that surprising. As a consequence, however, the weekend had the feeling of a family reunion, a church homecoming, or, perhaps more appropriately, a convention of sci-fi fans, dog breeders, or lunchbox-shaped salt-and-pepper shaker set collectors, at which people who share common passions and friendships come together along with their families to visit and get reacquainted. The Tribute Artist World Championship competition felt much more like a friendly gathering than a heated contest, with contestants comparing notes on jumpsuits, hairstyles, and dance moves, and sharing family photos along with details of what they had seen and done since the last time they were together.

This is not to say that tribute artist competitions are not important, because they clearly are. In addition to the purse offered to the winner at Elvis Expo 2004, the top four contestants were also offered a chance to perform extended sets with the house band (the excellent ExPense Account Showband) and have the performance digitally recorded. This, along with the publicity and bragging rights, are no doubt important to struggling performers who hope to improve their opportunities as wedding singers and cruise-ship entertainers. Winning Elvis Expo 2004 would not only make one a little richer, it could potentially open a lot of doors.

If the truth were told, each of the thirty plus Elvis tribute artists who took part in Elvis Expo 2004 in Las Vegas were probably there for a whole host of personal, idiosyncratic reasons. For some of them victory was everything, for others, the simple chance to be with people who share their calling was enough. One, an impersonator by the name of Steve Cates, made it clear that while he wanted to win, victory was far less important than the opportunity to perform with a professional band, gain hints and suggestions from other Elvis tribute artists (ETAs), and practice his craft in front of a very friendly audience.

Cates is probably typical of the average ETA. He performs as Elvis for a small fee at weddings and private parties and otherwise continues his day job. Elvis Expo 2004 was his first competition and it was clear that he was simply excited to be in Las Vegas with other Elvis fans. He seems committed to his craft but not ready or able to totally immerse himself in the lifestyle. For example, Cates has grown Elvis-style sideburns but he has not yet dyed his hair black. Likewise, he dresses in custom-made jumpsuits, but he had them made by a local tailor and not by a company that specializes in reproductions. Without the dyed hair and the reproduction jumpsuits, Cates only has one foot in the door. Unfortunately, defects in his costume marred his performance, as his belt buckle continued to pop open whenever he moved the wrong way, an occurrence that Cates managed with dignity and humor, referring to it as a 'wardrobe malfunction.'

The question of how committed one is willing to be to Elvis impersonation was indeed an issue that seemed to be of some importance to the ETAs. For example, Bernie Bennings, a blond from Austria who claims to be recognized as the best Elvis impersonator in Europe, made quite a big deal out of the fact that he had not dyed his hair and was not going to wear a wig for his performance. 'I am not Elvis,' he astutely observed, 'I am an entertainer.' Indeed, Bennings has something of a European following for his performance of both his own signature style of pop music, and for his Elvis impersonation acts. Unlike most impersonators, Bennings is a professional recording artist. True to his word, Bennings did offer up a very entertaining set of songs that earned him the right to appear in the final round and he did so as a blond. Apparently the pressure of the competition got to him, however, because during his performance for the finals he appeared on stage in a very bad Elvis wig. Unfortunately, this was not enough to win. Perhaps the judges, like myself, liked him better as a blond. One wonders if Bennings's last-minute change of heart was the result of a desire to complete the illusion and look more like Elvis, or a plan to demonstrate to the judges that he was a seriously committed tribute artist? Either way, Bennings, like Cates and most of the other tribute artists I talked to, did not seem driven by anything that I would call religious motivations, unless we really want to broaden our definition of religion to include the Miss America Pageant as a religious phenomenon. My experience within the hardcore Elvis tribute artist community lasted only a weekend, however, and I am certain that there is much that I missed. Perhaps those with deeper experience would see it differently.

Being Elvis

While there have been journalistic accounts from inside the Elvis tribute artist community, such as *I, Elvis: Confessions of a Counterfeit King* by William McCranor Henderson, author of the novel *Stark Raving Elvis*, and *Impersonating Elvis* by Leslie Rubinowski, the best looks at the ETA community come from the inside and are written by people with a personal history that is connected with Elvis impersonation. For example, Pamela Thomas-Williams's book *Elvis Lives: The Business of Being Elvis* presents an intimate and familiar look at the people who are a part of the Elvis impersonator phenomenon. Indeed, Thomas-Williams is not only an insider in the impersonator community, she also believes that Elvis is very much alive and that while he has never himself entered an impersonator contest he really enjoys seeing good impersonations done by others. This is not surprising, Thomas-Williams seems to argue, because Elvis enjoyed watching impersonations of himself before his death/disappearance. In addition to Elvis's appreciation of Andy Kaufman, Thomas-Williams also reports that Elvis enjoyed the work of such early impersonators as Rick Saucedo, who began his act in 1972, and Douglas Roy, who had Elvis join him on stage in 1976. In recounting the story of Elvis's interaction with impersonators, Thomas-Williams seems to be evoking the blessings of Elvis upon the tribute artist phenomenon.

Tribute artists also seek the blessings of Elvis upon their enterprise through what might be described loosely as a kind of apostolic succession. It is important that individuals who knew and worked with Elvis approve of what they are doing. D. J. Fontana, Elvis's drummer, is called upon to play in tribute bands or to speak at banquets in honor of Elvis. The Jordanaires, the gospel vocal group who sang with Elvis, and the Sweet Inspirations, Elvis's female backing singers, often perform in venues associated with tribute artists. Likewise, the ExPense Account Showband, long-associated with performing Elvis material, is an integral part of many tribute artist venues.

Of course, most tribute artists cannot afford to hire a professional band for their wedding and night-club performances, which is precisely why performing in a competition can itself be a big boost for the impersonator. While some tribute artists do have their own bands, most use pre-recorded music provided for them by such businesses as King Tracks. The opportunity to perform with a band like the ExPense Account Showband, with ties to Elvis and expert knowledge of his music, grants an air of respectability and orthodoxy to the performance of the tribute artists.

Just as it is important for tribute artists to associate themselves with people who knew and worked with Elvis, so tribute artists must also seek to dress as authentically as possible. Thomas-Williams notes what any tribute artists knows: it is B&K Enterprises that offers the most authentic costumes and who has the most direct lineage to Presley himself. B&K claims to possess the original patterns used to make Elvis's wardrobe and permission from the original designers to use their work. B&K is owned by Butch and Kim Polston and has provided costumes for Hollywood movies and for some of the best-known tribute artists in the world. Their fees, usually in the thousands of dollars, buy not only a custom-fitted costume that is authentically Elvis, but also a level of credibility among fellow tribute artists and fans.

The importance of the costume, and the 'look' in general, of the Elvis tribute artist is reinforced in Rick Marino's wonderful book *Be Elvis! A Guide to Impersonating the King*. Marino is a twenty-year veteran of Elvis impersonation and respected in the community as one of the most professional and influential figures in that circle. Marino describes what he does in the following:

An incredible thing happens when I go from being Rick to being Elvis. When I'm in costume, everywhere I go, I *am* Elvis! And I can do almost anything I want to do.

In costume, I feel the power Elvis had, the overwhelming effect he possessed over people. I can go into almost any building without question, and people are just awe struck – I honestly believe I could almost walk right into the White House! (Marino 2000: 6)

This sense of transformation from ordinary Rick Marino to Elvis Presley is one that comes as the result of a great deal of effort. Rick insists that if one is going to dress, act, and perform like Elvis, one should do it as carefully and professionally as possible. With that in mind, his book offers advice on hair and makeup, creative costuming, preparing a show, getting the act on the road, and marketing and publicity. Marino carefully describes what kind of hair dye to use, temporary not permanent, and how to go about the dyeing process. He recommends real sideburns rather than the paste-on variety and insists that Elvis impersonators should be ready to wear makeup just like Elvis did. One trick employed by the King, and recommended by Marino, is the use of mascara to cover any gray on the sideburns (19).

Marino's costuming advice is equally as detailed, as is his overview of the different styles of clothing Elvis wore at different times in his career. From the 1950s 'Cat Clothes Era,' through the 1967–1970 'Black Leather and White Suit Era,' the 1971–1973 'Color Era,' and the 1973–1975 'Stud and Stone Era,' and finally to the1974–1977 'Embroidered Era.' One should always get measured for a good fit and not make the collars too tall or too floppy. Belts should be like Elvis's, four inches wide, with buckles five to six inches high by seven and a half inches wide. Marino writes, 'The "V" on the front neckline should start at the base of the sternum and only go wide to just on either side of the start of the collarbones. The fly should have a pant-style flap to cover on the left side' (33).

Likewise, Marino's performance advice is apt and to the point. Tribute artists should follow Elvis's lead and fast before performances. Marino even recommends not eating at all on the day of a show. If you have to eat, try a banana or an oatmeal cookie. But in no circumstances should you eat anything less than three hours before a performance. Use honey and lemon in hot tea, or a healthy diet of cough drops to keep your voice in shape. Don't overdo the movements on stage. Elvis did move a lot, but not constantly throughout a sixty-minute performance. Suggest moves and then cut them short and save the action for big numbers. Finally, Marino suggests, get an entourage. Find a group of men to escort you to and from stage to make yourself look more important than you are.

Of course, all of Marino's expert advice only works if an artist has a venue in which to perform. As Thomas-Williams notes, the impersonator contests are the primary contexts in which Elvis tribute artists can perform, network, learn, and perfect their art. Such contests occur with great regularity and offer many opportunities for impersonators to practice their craft in the presence of Elvis luminaries and to perfect the authenticity of their costumes and performances. The Images of the King contest held in Memphis every August during the annual observance of his death is arguably the most important of these contests.

In addition to the Memphis contest, an Elvis festival and impersonator contest is held each year in Colingwood, Ontario, Canada. The Collingwood Elvis Festival features Elvis tribute artists performing in local bars and nightclubs during the week and concludes with a competition held on a main stage in the heart of the town. The festival is also marked by a candlelight vigil at midnight and a Saturday morning Elvis Tribute Artist Parade.

The People's Choice Award Contest is held annually in Montreal, Canada, and sponsored by LadyLuckMusic.com, a company that produces an Elvis tribute artist radio show and maintains a tribute artist website. Other contests are held at Isle of Capri Casino locations around the USA, with final rounds at the casino in Lula, Mississippi. Likewise the Potowatami Casino in Milwaukee, Wisconsin sponsors an annual contest with performances taking place in the heart of the casino floor. Other smaller venues also exist, including the newly established Elvis Expo to be held annually in Las Vegas. Of course, though not a contest per se, every impersonator has his eyes on John Stuart's Legends in Concert at the Imperial Palace in Las Vegas, with both a road show and a home in Sin City. Stuart's Legends show offers the most talented impersonators the chance to perform their craft professionally. Legends is truly the top of the game, a place where almost any impersonator would like to find themselves. When Stuart dropped by Elvis Expo 2004, complete with an entourage and video recording equipment, you could feel every impersonator in the place hold their breath.

The artists themselves are members of various professional organizations, the most important being the Professional Elvis Impersonators Association, an organization that is part of the Elvis Entertainers Network. To be a member of this association, impersonators must submit a performance video, photographs of the performer in costume, and a biography. An interview with a representative of the organization is also required. Entrance into the organization provides access to a network of tribute artist professionals and provides the services of a talent agency, helping impersonators find local venues in which to perform.

From the perspectives offered by Thomas-Williams and Marino, Elvis impersonation appears to be clearly about show business and the accompanying fame and fortune and is organized accordingly in professional organizations and talent agencies. Marino's rules for impersonation *might* be read as modern-day Leviticus, providing instructions and guidelines for priestly attire and behavior, but it seems to this author to be no more religious than any other 'How To' book on the market, whether about tax preparation, college admissions, or home decorating. Granted, the impersonators' quest to associate themselves with Elvis Presley by associating themselves with people who knew and worked with Elvis, and their emphasis upon authenticity and attention to detail may be traits that they share with certain religious communities, though by focusing on these traits alone we might be forced to draw the circle of religion a bit too large, for the same characteristics appear among American Civil War reenactors and collectors of model trains. Likewise, while the idea that by impersonating Elvis they are making the absent celebrity present to his fans might lead us to take impersonation as a kind of incarnation, in which the impersonator serves as a priest who mediates between the people and the spirit of Elvis, one wonders if Elvis impersonation might be closer to what an actor does on stage than what a priest does at the altar. There is nothing in Elvis impersonation itself, even authentically detailed impersonation, that alone would warrant a classification of this phenomenon as a religious one.

However, the fact that Elvis impersonators have become associated with, and even officiate at, a cultural ritual usually associated with religion is significant. So long as impersonators remain on stage, even when they perform at weddings and funerals, their religious function is questionable. However, when they assume the mantle of minister or rabbi and actually officiate at wedding ceremonies, it seems clear that an explicitly religious element is at play.

Well, perhaps not all that clear.

— Impersonators and Priests —

Elvis Weddings

When I dropped by the Graceland Wedding Chapel in Las Vegas, a chapel where the Elvis-themed weddings are often officiated by Norm Jones, an Elvis impersonator who is also an ordained minister, Peggy Johnson, one of the owners, seemed genuinely surprised that I would be researching the topic of Elvis and religion. Even when I explicitly noted that weddings are often religious events and weddings at her 'chapel' were often Elvis themed, she didn't seem to know what to say. It was as if she had not herself made the connection that the person of Elvis Presley in the form of an Elvis impersonator was playing any sort of religious or priestly role.

Perhaps one of the reasons for this response can be found in the history of Las Vegas in regard to both weddings and Elvis Presley. Indeed, quick, informal weddings are as much a part of Las Vegas culture as is Elvis himself. As Susan Marg points out in her wonderful book *Las Vegas Weddings: A Brief History, Celebrity Gossip, Everything Elvis, and the Complete Chapel Guide*, weddings have been a part of the identity of Vegas since its founding. In the early part of the twentieth century divorce and remarriage was made easy in Las Vegas to satisfy the demands of relocated men attracted to the area because of job opportunities and who had left their wives behind. Later, as California placed tighter and tighter restrictions on divorce and marriage, Las Vegas became legendary as a place for Californians to go for either a quick divorce or a quick marriage. Celebrities from Hollywood made the place famous nationwide as the place to get married. Wedding chapels sprang up alongside casinos. According to Marg, more than one hundred and twenty thousand couples have tied the knot in Las Vegas since the year 2000. Nearly fifty thousand more have participated in the renewal of vows in that time. 'This means about 5 percent of all weddings performed in the United States in a given year take place in a county that accounts for less than 0.5 percent of the population of the country' (Marg 2004: 1).

Elvis himself was married in Las Vegas at the Aladdin Hotel and Casino, though he is probably more associated in Las Vegas with Ann-Margret than with his wife, Priscilla, because of their roles in the movie *Viva Las Vegas*, the title song of which would become the unofficial theme song of the Nevada town. Likewise, of course, Elvis's later Las Vegas shows produced an indelible image of the King in white jumpsuit and cape. By the latter part of the twentieth century, Vegas could be summed up in three words: gambling, wedding chapels, and Elvis.

It should come as no surprise, then, that Elvis would become associated with weddings in Las Vegas, just as casinos have embraced the wedding chapel business. Elvis is, after all, part of the Las Vegas image. According to Marg, the Graceland Wedding Chapel received four to five requests every month for an Elvis wedding as early as 1977. This number has increased to four to five requests a day (197). For many people, part of what it means to get married in Las Vegas is to evoke the image of Elvis Presley. In this sense Elvis is around as a source of ironic kitsch, or as a nod to the flash of Vegas culture. Elvis makes the weddings fun and lighthearted. His image sums up what it means to be married in Sin City. It might very well be, therefore, that the presence of an Elvis impersonator at a Las Vegas wedding ceremony is without direct religious connotations and that Peggy Johnson is right to be surprised that this author would bring up the connection.

However, when reading Marg's descriptions of Elvis wedding ceremonies, it is clear that we might not want to put away the religious hypothesis too quickly. For example,

Marg describes Elvis-themed weddings held at the Viva Las Vegas Wedding Chapel. In these ceremonies an Elvis impersonator may conduct the ceremony and sing. The impersonator is not an ordained minister, so the official part of the service has to be conducted by someone else, in this case the Reverend Ron Rogers of the Salvation Army, who often performs traditional (meaning non-Elvis) ceremonies at the chapel as well. Interestingly, the Reverend Rogers performs his contribution to the Elvis service offstage with the bride and groom and away from the guests, thus reinforcing the appearance that it is the impersonator himself who performs the wedding. It would seem, therefore, that there is something significant about being married by Elvis, as opposed to just having him at your wedding.

Indeed, Marg notes that Marcello Dinicolantonio, the resident Elvis impersonator at the Viva Las Vegas Chapel, is himself in training to become an ordained minister, a distinction held by only one other Elvis impersonator, Norm Jones, of the Graceland Wedding Chapel. Jones, however, while performing the roles of both Elvis impersonator and minister refuses to combine the two roles, and will not perform marriages while dressed as Elvis. Dinicolantonio has no such worries, though, and plans to perform weddings in their entirety while impersonating Elvis. In the meantime he is content to allow an ordained minister to put the official stamp on a service that clearly already belongs to him, to Elvis.

This is Marg's description of one of Viva Las Vegas's Elvis weddings:

> Penny and Sean have elected to have the Elvis Special, one of Viva Las Vegas' most popular wedding packages. 'Elvis is like a member of our family,' Penny explains, echoing the feeling of Elvis fans through the decades. The ceremony is a mix of the traditional with the novel. Most couples, like these newlyweds, dress up for the

occasion, yet they walk down the aisle while a man who looks and sounds like Elvis sings *Can't Help Falling in Love*. After promising 'to love, honor, and cherish each other,' the couple dances together for the first time as husband and wife while Elvis sings *Love Me Tender*. And after rings are exchanged and blessed by the reverend, Elvis sings the chapel's theme song, *Viva Las Vegas*. The setting is churchlike, with light flooding through stained glass windows and flowers decorating the pews. Yet it is Elvis standing at the altar. (211–212)

With all of this in mind, I am still not willing to grant my endorsement of the priestly hypothesis as the best interpretation of the impersonator phenomenon, however. Even when Elvis impersonators take on a clearly religious role it is evident that many other factors are at work. Though it is notoriously difficult, if not outright impossible, to tease out causes from effects in such contexts, it would seem to me that there is a viable alternative to the impersonator as priest metaphor available to explain the Elvis wedding phenomenon. Strausbaugh and Harrison would no doubt say that Elvis weddings, that is, weddings officiated by Elvis impersonators, offer clear evidence of the religious/priestly nature of the Elvis impersonator phenomenon as a whole. It is possible, however, that this is to put the cart before the horse. After considering the history of Las Vegas wedding chapels and the deep connections between the city and Elvis Presley, it seems reasonable to surmise that Elvis has become associated with weddings simply because they both are such an important part of Las Vegas history and culture. Nothing says authentic Las Vegas wedding like having Elvis sing, or walk the bride down the aisle, or even officiate. In this case, instead of saying that Elvis impersonators have become associated with Las Vegas weddings because of the priestly nature of impersonation, we might say that Elvis impersonators appear priestly because of their association with Las Vegas weddings. But of course, just when it looks like we have it figured out . . .

Elvis Chaplains

Though perhaps an anomaly in the world of Elvis impersonators, Joseph Thomas of Anniston, Alabama, might just
indicate an expansion of the priestly role for Elvis impersonators. The following is from the June 26, 2004
Huntsville Times from Huntsville, Alabama.

Elvis has not left hospital building
Impersonator has patients all shook up as new chaplain
By Greg Garrison
Religion News Service

Anniston – Elvis impersonator Joseph Thomas was the
first person to undergo open-heart bypass surgery at
Anniston's Regional Medical Center.

'They treated me like the king I am,' he said.

Now, Thomas walks around the hospital as a volunteer chaplain wearing his colorful jumpsuits, lamb-chop
sideburns and dangling sterling silver jewelry, saying
'Thank you very much.'

Thomas said when he tells patients about his successful surgery, 'their faith and hope skyrocket.'

Sometimes he'll sing a song to life their spirits.

'When I sing, I remind them of Elvis,' Thomas said.

Thomas, who performs under the stage name 'Rock-
ing Ronnie Romance,' had quadruple bypass heart
surgery last December. In April out of gratitude, he
began working as a volunteer chaplain at the hospital,
visiting as many as 25 patients a day on Mondays and
Fridays.

Thomas said he was baptized at age 8 in the East
Point, Georgia, Church of God and was ordained at age
16 at a church in rural Alabama. He said he played
drums and piano with gospel groups as a teenager.

'When I was doing gospel, at 15 or 16 years old, people
were calling me Elvis,' he said. 'I began to see it and hear
it myself. It's just a natural thing.'

In 1984 he began performing Elvis Presley songs at
corporate parties. In 1993, he moved to Nashville, Ten-

nessee and staff members from Country Music Television flagged him down on the street, he said.

They asked him to do an appearance on the network's 1994 country music video countdown, posing as a bus driver who thinks he's Elvis and kidnaps singers Pam Tillis and Marty Stuart. That show led to numerous television commercials.

In 1995, Thomas went to Graceland, Presley's mansion in Memphis, Tennessee. People began following him around and speculated that Elvis had faked his own death, he said.

'The more I told them I wasn't Elvis, the more they believed I was,' he said. 'They would say, "We know you had to do what you had to do." I had women to stalk me and old men chasing me with cameras, grown men crying, saying "Elvis, please come back." They didn't want him to go. It's just hard for people to accept that Elvis died. If they seen anybody that reminds them of him, they get freaky.'

Though shorter than the real Elvis and more portly, the 45-year old Thomas said he has gotten used to attracting attention for his appearance.

'If I had a dollar every time somebody called me Elvis, Bill Gates would be my janitor,' Thomas said.

Thomas' gaudy jewelry includes a king's crown pendant and a Star of David, both sterling silver. He also wears fancy watches and rings and an eagle bolo tie. He has an assortment of suits, including one with a white cape.

'There's been a mixed response from our staff,' said Chaplain Jim Wilson, head of chaplaincy at the hospital. 'He does wear what amounts to a stage costume when he makes rounds. Some people are put off by that. He does have lovely suits. They are well-tailored. He's a sharp individual.'

Staff at the hospital don't want to be cruel but are concerned about an Elvis impersonator becoming the mascot of the cardiology department, Wilson said.

'I have a concern about his being the prototype for our chaplaincy and our heart program,' Wilson said. 'It's a

serious thing for us. It's a major step. I've only had negative feedback from one patient. I've had negative
feedback from the staff.'

But Wilson said Thomas seems to be a hit while making rounds. 'He seems to be capable in his dealing with
the patients.'

Hospital spokeswoman Susan Williamson said there
are no plans to force Elvis to leave the building.

Thomas hopes the hospital lets him stay as a volunteer chaplain. All he can do is offer his characteristic
gratitude. 'Thank you,' he said as he finished meeting
with a newspaper reporter. 'Thank you very much.'

— Conclusion —

Well, there you have it. Just as my trip to Memphis failed
to turn up the gathering place of some strange new Elvis
cult, so my trip to Las Vegas failed to turn up any clear
examples of Elvis ministers or priests. Oh, don't get me
wrong, I found a lot of people dressed in white, repeating
the words of a deceased idol, and laying hands, and
scarves, and lips upon an adoring crowd. I'm just not sure
that any of the participants, either performers or observers,
would describe any of this activity in religious terms. It is
show business, it is performance, it is rock 'n' roll, it is sexy,
it is hilarious, but it is not necessarily religious.

Indeed, if Elvis tribute artists were forced to identify the
essence of their craft, I have no doubt that they would use
essentially show business terminology to do so. What they
do, whether performing as wedding singers, or at small-
town Labor Day festivities, or in competition with other
tribute artists, is simply a very specialized type of entertainment. They are not quite singers, not quite actors, but some
sort of strange mixture of both. They usually don't attract
large crowds, their only real hope of making any money is

to get a full-time gig in Vegas, but, unlike other areas of the entertainment business, Elvis impersonation is relatively easy to get into. The material, the look, and the audience is already there.

Most of the people I have talked to say they impersonate Elvis because it is fun. An Elvis impersonator, unlike countless other lounge singing acts, is an instant celebrity. (Hey, look, it's Elvis!) But, of course, they, and the audience, know that they are not the King. They know that they are not as good looking, or as talented, or as charismatic. For Elvis impersonators, however, these are not limits. Since no impersonator is the real McCoy, everyone is free to present only 'passable' versions of Elvis's look, sound, and style. Those moments when the distance between Elvis and impersonator is the greatest, as when one impersonator's huge belt buckle kept popping open during the performance, are not times for embarrassment or shame. They simply show what everyone already knows. (Hey, look, it's not Elvis!) The irony is lost on no one.

And for all of those Elvis weddings in Las Vegas? Again, it is not that the presence of Elvis makes the ceremonies religious, it is rather that the presence of Elvis makes the ceremonies Las Vegas. Quick weddings, and quicker divorces, flashy costumes and lights, everything in excess and in bad taste: this is Las Vegas. Likewise, in so many ways: this is Elvis. This is why the proprietor of Graceland Chapel looked at me as if I was nuts when I said I was interested in Elvis and religion. In Las Vegas, religion is really the last thing on anyone's mind, even at a wedding.

And Joseph Thomas, of Anniston, Alabama? Well, Elvis and religion certainly seem to be intertwined in that one man's life. But, that should probably not strike anyone as odd. After all, ministers are people too. They have many of the same interests, mainstream or idiosyncratic, as the rest of us. A minister who dresses as Elvis is not really any stranger than the medical lab tech, the high-school teacher, the electrician, or the bus driver who dresses as Elvis. Please note: I am not claiming that it isn't strange, a little out of the ordinary, but that it is no stranger for a minister than for anyone else.

So, if I couldn't find an Elvis cult gathering annually at Graceland, and if I couldn't make myself see Elvis impersonators as priests, just exactly where, if anywhere, was I going to find Elvis religion? If not in Memphis or Las Vegas, then where? Ah, of course, Hollywood!

3

Elvis in Film

Violent Visions, Ambiguous Angels

— Elvis Movies —

I can't remember ever watching an Elvis Presley movie from start to finish until I was compelled to do so by the needs of the present research. This seems rather odd when I consider it because, first of all, Elvis made a lot of movies, and second, they are played on cable television at all times of the day and night. As a matter of fact, the most ubiquitous visual images of Elvis are the images produced by Hollywood. The thirty-one films that Elvis starred in provide indelible images of the young star, who, if not always at his musical peak, was almost always presented smiling, trim, and Technicolor vibrant. In the course of this astounding output of visual images, which date from *Love Me Tender* in 1956 to *Change of Habit* in 1969, (more than two films per year on average) Elvis was called upon to do little more than play himself and, of course, sing. At times, this formula worked to good effect, as in 1957's *Jailhouse Rock* in which Elvis portrays a hot-headed and troubled ex-con who is able to channel his anger and aggression into riveting musical performances. At other times, or shall we say most of the time, the results were not as spectacular. The more his character's troubled anger was hidden away the less interesting the films usually turned out to be.

There is, oddly enough, no single cinematic character that stands out from all of his movies, except of course Elvis himself. Before they are westerns, comedies, action films, or musicals, these films are Elvis Movies. They comprise a genre all their own. They are, plain and simple, vehicles for Elvis. As such, their success or failure as films has more to do with the look and sound of their lead than with plot, character, acting or direction. What matters in these films, what makes them continue to be watched, and broadcast and rebroadcast, is the simple fact that Elvis is in them. They are Elvis Movies. The character that the audience is interested in is Elvis himself, regardless of the fictional name or profession Elvis is effecting at the time.

It might come as some surprise that films have continued to place Elvis as a central character long after his death, and that Elvis Movies, as a genre, continue to be made, though with decidedly less innocence and naïveté than was common in the movies actually starring Elvis Presley. The posthumous movies that feature Elvis as a character do so with the knowledge of how things turned out for the King. It is precisely because of the absence of Elvis Presley as a living and breathing character that some of these films present Elvis in a spiritual or religious context. Though Elvis cannot be with us in the flesh he can be with us in the spirit.

For the sake of research I made a trip to the video rental store, I popped a little popcorn, sprinkled it with salt from my Elvis lunchbox and thermos salt-and-pepper shaker set, and settled in to watch Elvis movies, old and new.

Mystery Train

One of the earliest films to evoke the posthumous character of Elvis was 1989's *Mystery Train*. Jim Jarmusch's film about overnight boarders in a Memphis hotel follows three sets of characters through stories that intersect only tangentially, but which are all tangled up with Elvis. First introduced are two young Japanese tourists, Jun and Mitzuko, who have embarked on a rock 'n' roll pilgrimage to Memphis. Their strange trek across Memphis, carrying an enormous suitcase between them, places the characters against a stark landscape of urban blight and decay. At night they check into a hotel and find a portrait of Elvis hanging on the wall of their room, like a religious icon, or Salman's *Head of Christ*. Mitzuko, clearly a devotee of Elvis, carries a scrapbook of images of Elvis's face throughout history, revealed in a visage of the Buddha and in the profile of the Statue of Liberty. Elvis's haunting 'Blue Moon', recorded at Sun Studios right there in Memphis, plays on a local radio station. As morning comes, the couple is startled by the sound of gunfire but, without any explanation of this, the scene shifts and the next set of characters is introduced.

This time we meet a widowed Italian woman by the name of Luisa who, while flying the body of her deceased husband home to Italy, becomes stranded in Memphis. When she stops at a newsstand to buy a newspaper she is browbeaten by the vendor into buying a stack of magazines she does not want. At a diner, she is accosted by a man who tells her a strange story about picking up the ghost of Elvis as a hitchhiker who then sent him to this place to meet her. She pays him $20 for a comb that 'belonged to Elvis' just to get him to leave. He follows her from the diner, however, and she is forced to duck into a hotel to escape. She ends up sharing a hotel room with a local woman who cannot afford a room of her own. Their room is also adorned with the image of Elvis. 'Blue Moon' plays on the radio. As her roommate goes to sleep Luisa is startled to see an apparition of Elvis, confused and apologetic for being in the wrong room. In the morning, the strange gunshot rings out.

The scene shifts once again and the audience is introduced to Johnny, a drunk and violent Englishman who hangs out in an African-American bar. His black friends call him 'Elvis.' After leaving the bar with two other men, Johnny surprises his companions by robbing a liquor store and murdering the clerk. They then drive around all night only to end up in the same hotel as the movie's other protagonists. Taking a wrecked room for their hideout, the portrait of Elvis watches over them even there. 'Blue Moon' plays on the radio. A suicidal Johnny fires a gunshot, hitting one of his companions. The movie ends with the main characters leaving Memphis at the end of this night in which they had all been in the presence of the King.

In *Mystery Train*, Jarmusch clearly evokes religious imagery in his development of the Elvis character who, even though he only appears on screen for a few brief seconds and then only as a ghostly apparition, is central to the story. Pilgrims come to his holy city to visit holy sites in his honor. In scrapbook images, Elvis is portrayed as incarnate divinity down through the ages, giving perhaps a promise of his rebirth yet again. His face is that of an icon, an ancestor passed to the other side, who watches over the living. His voice, in the haunting 'Blue Moon', speaks as if from the grave. He appears in the likeness of a hitchhiker and sends his apostle on a divine mission. His name is given and taken by other men, conferring his presence even after his death. He appears in a vision, like an angel. This Elvis Movie, like *Jailhouse Rock* and *Girls, Girls, Girls*, features Elvis as a character. It just so happens that Elvis is dead. His presence is spiritual, rather than physical, mediated like the presence of Jesus, through icons and visions.

Yet, and this is very important, Jarmusch's spiritual Elvis is a complex and darkly ambiguous figure. The Memphis that remains his home is a broken shell of a city. His icon hangs in third-rate motel rooms, scenes of violence and sorrow. The mission his apostle claims is a mission of violence. The one who is given and takes his name is controlled by alcohol and gunplay. When Elvis appears in a vision he is confused, lost and uncertain. Perhaps, Jarmusch seems to suggest, after his death Elvis can give us more truth than while he lived. Instead of the Technicolor images of Elvis Movies starring Elvis Presley, where violence is mostly harmless, people are mostly good looking, and misogyny is fun for everyone, *Mystery Train* shows us the dark side of Memphis, the serious side of violence, and the danger faced by women. Now Elvis is no longer a brash youth with striking good looks and words of truth, but rather his spirit is as lost as our own. Of course, how else could it be, considering what we know about his end? The spirit of Elvis watches over a city broken by poverty and violence. In his name men threaten women and murder other men. His appearance brings no clear direction from beyond the grave.

Wild at Heart

David Lynch's *Wild at Heart* (1990) offers up many of the same themes, though with less overt religious imagery and more overt violence. I should also add that it has less overt reference to Elvis himself. Indeed, except for Nicolas Cage's dead-on impersonation of Presley's singing voice and his sometimes passable imitation of Presley's idiosyncracies, there is little that makes this an Elvis Movie. This very absence of Elvis, however, is one of the driving forces of the film. Because Cage does channel Elvis, and precisely because he does so with such mixed results, the viewer is constantly reminded of Elvis and reminded that Cage is not Elvis. If Cage's Sailor is Elvis incarnate, reincarnated if you will, then it is as an inexact incarnation. The Elvis character of *Jailhouse Rock* commits manslaughter in a moment of passion, just as Cage's Elvis character does. He too goes to prison and is released into the arms of a girl. But *Wild at Heart* is no *Jailhouse Rock*. It is a David Lynch-Elvis Movie and, as such, is filled with fat strippers, gratuitous violence, and strange allusions to, of all things, *The Wizard of Oz*. On a much darker level than in *Mystery Train*, Elvis's spirit, his reincarnated presence, reveals to the viewer a world of absurd violence. Surprisingly, however, in this world of death and deceit it is the spirit of Elvis that is also able to reveal hope and love. While Cage's impersonations of Elvis's mannerisms are never exactly on target, his renditions of Elvis's songs 'Love Me' and 'Love Me Tender' are quite good. 'Love Me Tender', Sailor tells Lula, is the one song he is saving to sing to his wife. True to his word, and to the audience's expectations, he delivers the song to her as the closing credits roll. It is in these songs, more so than anything in else, that the viewer is offered a glimpse of the redemption to be found in the love affair between Sailor and Lula.

True Romance

True Romance (1993) continues the themes found in *Mystery Train* and *Wild at Heart*, sometimes seeming to lift elements from these two earlier movies for its own use. This movie, directed by Tony Scott from a script by Quentin Tarantino, follows the adventures of Clarence, who falls in love with a hooker by the name of Alabama and ends up in a great deal of trouble. Clarence, we are shown right from the beginning, is a big fan of Elvis. It is important that his favorite Elvis Movie is the atypical *Jailhouse Rock*. Clarence says,

> In *Jailhouse Rock* he's everything rockabilly's about. I mean he is rockabilly: mean, surly, nasty, rude. In that movie he couldn't give a fuck about anything except rockin' and rollin', livin' fast, dyin' young, and leaving a good-looking corpse. I love that scene where after he's made it big he's throwing a big cocktail party, and all these highbrows are there, and he's singing, 'Baby You're So Square . . . Baby, I Don't Care.' Now, they got him dressed like a dick. He's wearing these stupid-lookin' pants, this horrible sweater. Elvis ain't no sweater boy. I even think they got him wearin' penny loafers. Despite all that shit, all the highbrows at the party, big house, the stupid clothes, he's still a rude-lookin' motherfucker. I'd watch that hillbilly and I'd want to be him so bad. Elvis looked good. I'm no fag, but Elvis was good-lookin'. He was fuckin' prettier than most women. I always said if I ever had to fuck a guy . . . I mean had too 'cause my life depended on it . . . I'd fuck Elvis.

After his marriage to Alabama, Clarence is obsessed with really freeing her from her pimp and considers going to him to claim her belongings. The following exchange takes place in a bathroom between Clarence and a vision of Elvis, portrayed by Val Kilmer:

ELVIS: Can you live with it?
CLARENCE: Live with what?
ELVIS: With that son-of-a-bitch walkin' around breathin' the same air as you? And gettin' away with it every day. Are you haunted?
CLARENCE: Yeah.
ELVIS: You wanna get unhaunted?
CLARENCE: Yeah.

ELVIS: Then shoot 'em. Shoot 'em in the face. And feed that boy to the dogs.

CLARENCE: I can't believe what you're tellin' me.

ELVIS: I ain't tellin' ya nothin'. I'm just sayin' what I'd do.

CLARENCE: You'd really do that?

ELVIS: He don't got no right to live.

CLARENCE: Look, Elvis, he is hauntin' me. He doesn't deserve to live. And I do want to kill him. But I don't wanna go to jail for the rest of my life.

ELVIS: I don't blame you.

CLARENCE: If I thought I could get away with it —

ELVIS: Killin' 'em's the hard part. Gettin' away with it's the easy part. Whaddaya think the cops do when a pimp's killed? Burn the midnight oil tryin' to find who done it? They couldn't give a flyin' fuck if all the pimps in the whole wide world took two in the back of the fuckin' head. If you don't get caught at the scene with the smokin' gun in your hand, you got away with it. Clarence, I like ya. Always have, always will.

Following Elvis's sinister advice, Clarence murders the pimp, steals a suitcase full of narcotics, and embarks on a violent odyssey with Alabama. *True Romance* offers up Elvis as a ghostly vision, reminiscent of *Mystery Train*, with all the violence of *Wild at Heart*. Elvis appears to Clarence in a vision that encourages him to give in to his darkest nature. He speaks with a vulgar vocabulary that one could not imagine from Elvis Presley in that earlier sort of Elvis Movie. He advocates not a bar-room brawl, but bullets in the back of the head. The spirit of Elvis that is revealed to Clarence is macabre, and though his obscene advice does result in a happy ending, the path to that happiness is bloody and mean.

3000 Miles to Graceland

The trail of violence left in the wake of Elvis's passing continues in *3000 Miles to Graceland* (2001). Here there are no ghostly appearances by Elvis, though the character of Elvis is clearly present throughout. Kevin Costner and Kurt Russell play former cellmates who plan the heist of a Las Vegas casino. Attempting the robbery during an Elvis impersonator convention, the ex-cons and their accomplices disguise themselves in the ostentatious rhinestone jumpsuits favored by Elvis in his later years and by impersonators everywhere. A violent shoot-out ends with a successful robbery, only to have Costner's character turn a gun on the other members of his team and leave them for dead. Like Elvis, and of course Jesus, Russell's character (remember, Russell played Elvis in an earlier biopic, *Elvis*, in 1979) returns from the dead and sets out to reclaim the money. The money swaps back and forth between the two protagonists who, we are told in a subplot involving police investigators, have both claimed to be the illegitimate sons of Elvis Presley. After Costner's 'bad' Elvis dies in a bloody shoot-out with the police, Russell's 'good' Elvis finally gets what he has wanted all along, the chance to claim his inheritance, a boat named *Graceland* left to him by his father.

As in earlier posthumous Elvis Movies this is a tale of violence, greed, and death. And, as in those films, Elvis's presence is felt most keenly in his absence. In *3000 Miles to Graceland* Elvis is the departed father. The protagonists each claim to be his son, but only one of them is true. The true son is betrayed and murdered only to rise again to seek justice. In the end, after much suffering, this justice is attained and the true son receives his inheritance. Though perhaps less visible than in other films in this genre, the presence of Elvis is arguably more important. Elvis is not simply present in a reincarnate form, as in *Wild at Heart*, or as a ghostly apparition, as in *Mystery Train* and *True Romance*. Rather, Elvis is a father and, because of his death and because he is ELVIS, a father of a rather grand sort. Indeed, Elvis drives the actions of the hero, not as a causal influence, as we see in *True Romance*, but as a teleological goal. This movie is the record of a son's violent journey to the father, a bloody journey to Graceland.

Six-String Samurai

A similar theme is to be found in 1998's *Six-String Samurai*, an apocalyptic martial arts film set in an alternative reality where a 1950s nuclear holocaust destroyed most of civilization and left Elvis as the monarch of 'Lost Vegas.' After the death of the King, everyone, including Jeffrey Falcon's Buddy, a 1950s rocker with a samurai blade hidden in his guitar, sets off to Vegas to claim the throne. The onscreen violence in this film is the sort of violence found in martial arts movies and comic books, fun to look at and improbably clean. The real violence in this film, however, is, like Elvis, mostly posthumous: the violence of the past is far greater than the violence of the present. Civilization is in ruins in the aftermath of humanity's great apocalyptic war. Consequently, the violence of swords and bows and arrows appears quaint and harmless against this larger background.

Not insignificantly, the character of Elvis dwells in this background. He is unseen, his throne never revealed on screen, his kingdom mostly invisible. As such, King Elvis has as much, or more, of a presence than the onscreen hero Buddy and his kid sidekick. These characters remain undeveloped. Buddy is the six-string samurai, with one goal in mind, to be King of Lost Vegas. He is kinder than he looks, however, and when he befriends a small boy we are left in little doubt that, while Buddy may be all business on the outside, on the inside he is kind and caring. There is nothing really interesting about Buddy as a character, just as there is little more to the movie itself than fight scenes interspersed with cute scenes with the kid. Indeed, the elements of interest in this film are its apocalyptic setting in a world of posthumous violence, and the motivation of the characters, good and bad, to make it to Lost Vegas to claim the throne of the posthumous King. Just as the apocalypse provides the setting, Elvis provides the motivation for the journey.

Finding Graceland

Yet another Elvis Movie with a journey as the central motif, *Finding Graceland* differs from both *3000 Miles to Graceland* and *Six-String Samurai* in that violence is not a central theme, and Elvis appears as a living, breathing character, albeit one that bears no resemblance whatsoever to Elvis Presley. Jonathon Schaech portrays a man in mourning for the loss of his wife; he picks up a hitchhiker, played by Harvey Keitel, who is traveling to Graceland. The hitchhiker isn't just an Elvis fan, however, but claims to be the King himself on his way back home after an absence of many years.

Along the way, in addition to seeing Keitel perform 'Suspicious Minds' in an Elvis jumpsuit, the audience is first led to believe that Keitel really is Elvis, then that he is a delusional fanatic, and, in the end, that he is the real thing after all. It seems that Elvis, after dropping out, began to travel around and help people, showing strangers what they had to live for. He is an angel of mercy, touching lives wherever he goes. By reading the subtle cries for help in the faces he encounters he is able to save them and remind them to 'remember the King.' This movie leaves the viewer wondering what is real and what is fantasy. Is this Elvis or is it a deluded man just doing the good work of the King? Does it really matter?

Heartbreak Hotel

Heartbreak Hotel is Chris Columbus's 1988 film about a fictional kidnapping of Elvis Presley by teenagers in Ohio after a 1972 concert. The kidnapping is masterminded by a teen whose mother (Tuesday Weld, who starred with Elvis Presley in *Wild in the Country* and was romantically involved with him) has been a fan of Elvis since she was a teenager and has become mired in depression and alcoholism. The gift of Elvis, played by David Keith, is meant to be a birthday surprise, and it is. In the course of a few days, and with the help of Elvis, the normal Ohio family learns to love and enjoy life again, mom overcomes her crises, and the teenager plays with Elvis in a high-school talent competition. The movie isn't only about Elvis making others' dreams come true however, for the King himself learns some valuable lessons, like how to reclaim his youth and once again rock and roll.

Bubba Ho-tep

Like *Finding Graceland*, *Bubba Ho-tep* (2002) responds to the decline and death of Elvis Presley by imagining that Elvis escaped from the pressure of life at the top before the tragedy occurred. By changing places with an Elvis impersonator, Elvis became Sebastian Haff, and Sebastian became Elvis. Sebastian Haff, unfortunately, also became a drug addict and died at Graceland, trapping the real Elvis in his life. Or at least this is what the main character Sebastian/Elvis seems to believe.

The movie begins in the present day when Elvis, as Sebastian, and played by Bruce Campbell, is living in a Texas nursing home after falling off stage and breaking his hip. Along with Elvis, John F. Kennedy is also a resident of the home, having, apparently, been forced from his old life by his enemies. JFK's complexion – he is played by Ozzie

Davis – is explained as a full body dye used to make him unrecognizable. The two reclaim their lost youth to do battle with an Egyptian mummy, a soul-sucker, who is preying on the souls of other residents of the home.

While, of course, this plot is played for laughs, the script is actually very character driven. Oddly enough, while *Finding Graceland* and *Heartbreak Hotel* try to present a tender and heroic image of Elvis, they both come off as sappy and laughable. *Bubba Ho-tep*, on the other hand, embraces the ironic quality of Elvis's personality and comes closest of all to presenting Elvis as a sympathetic, heroic character.

One of the most interesting things about Elvis Movies made after the death of Elvis Presley is the ways in which the films respond to the absence of Elvis. How is the character of Elvis to be present, considering the very real fact of Elvis's death? The movies that we have talked about in this chapter deliver the presence of Elvis in at least two ways. In many of these films, the death of Elvis is taken as a given, but the character of Elvis himself continues to influence the plot and the other characters. In other films, Elvis's death is denied and the character of Elvis is portrayed by another actor. The first type of film presents the deceased Elvis as the harbinger of violent visions, the latter presents him as an ambiguous angel.

— Violent Visions —

Whether in Hinduism's grand system of death and rebirth, where souls are continually reborn until they are able to achieve release in *moksha*, or in the notion common to western religions that individuals may live and act in the spirit of the deceased, a common response to death is to look for the deceased in the lives of the living. A belief in the reincarnation of the deceased, and of the incarnation of deities in the lives of individuals, is a central belief of many religions. It is, I believe, just such a religious vision that we can see in David Lynch's *Wild at Heart*. The presence of Elvis, as a reincarnate ancestor or an incarnate deity, is experienced through Cage's Sailor. Elvis lives in his attitude, his mannerisms, and his songs. Indeed, even though the film does not directly draw such lines of connection for the viewer, one cannot help but experience them. Sailor is Elvis, but, of course, he is not. The film itself evokes from the viewer a primitive religious response in that we can see the presence of Elvis in this other person. Elvis lives on after death for those who can see him in the character of Sailor.

In contrast, *Mystery Train* and *True Romance* are films that present encounters with Elvis beyond the grave through apparitions and visions. In *Mystery Train*, the character of Luisa encounters Elvis late at night as an apparition. The vision is unclear and undeveloped, dreamlike in its ambiguity. It might be as accurate to say that Luisa has seen a ghost as to say that she has experienced a vision. This ghost, this brief spiritual presence of one who is physically absent, is only one element in a rich religious tapestry. Much like visions of angels and deities reported around the world, this vision takes place in a holy city, the place of Elvis's death and the birthplace of rock 'n' roll, and the experience is had in the presence of icons and images. Together, apparition, icons, relics, and pilgrims evoke a spiritual encounter, evoke the spiritual presence, of Elvis.

Markedly different is the vision of Elvis in *True Romance*. Here the presence of Elvis comes devoid of the rich religious context found in *Mystery Train*. Elvis appears to Clarence in a bathroom in a form that is definitely more vision than apparition, more personal epiphany than ghost sighting. Elvis speaks directly to Clarence and encourages behavior that initiates the violent journey that is to follow.

Elvis appears to Clarence like Jesus to Paul on the road to Damascus and this appearance, like that earlier one, will change the course of a life.

The character of Elvis as deceased father/king in *3000 Miles to Graceland* and *Six-String Samurai* also serves to evoke the spiritual presence of the physically absent Elvis. In both films, presented as journeys filled with danger and adventure, the characters are motivated first and foremost by a desire to claim the inheritance that is – or, in the case of *Samurai*, may be – theirs. In both cases, the journey and the reward take on decidedly spiritual elements. Neither the physical boat named *Graceland* nor the temporal kingship of Lost Vegas really constitute the focus of the quests. Rather, both *Graceland* and Lost Vegas seem to stand for a new life for the main characters, both are representative of new beginnings and an escape from the violence that is central to their lives.

The violence of these two films is a common element in many of the Elvis Movies that we are considering. Indeed, while the five movies that we have just examined share the common element of transforming the physical absence of Elvis into a spiritual or religious presence, they also share the common element of violence. The role played by the character of Elvis in regard to this violence differs from film to film, however, and includes reactions that range from confusion to an outright advocacy of violence.

The first response, confusion and uncertainty, is seen in the response of Elvis in *Mystery Train*. In this film, the city of Memphis, home of Elvis's beloved Graceland, is presented as decaying and depressed. Visitors to the city are treated harshly by businessmen and residents. Icons to Elvis hang in seedy hotel rooms. Men use the memory of Elvis to approach and threaten women. Murder and robbery is committed without thought. Surely the spirit of Elvis, here in his own holy city, in an inn dedicated to his memory, among fans and devotees, will have some message to give in the midst of this violence. Surely, the King will bring words of peace. And yet, when Elvis does appear, as an apparition in a hotel room, he seems as bewildered by it all as the rest of us. He is kind and apologetic, but otherwise lost. Memphis, Jarmusch is saying, and America for that matter, is lost. Japanese tourists on a holy pilgrimage visit the holy city without receiving inspiration. Widows are accosted and threatened. Violence rules the night. The American dream, like Elvis, is dead, only an apparition, only a ghost. One does not come away from *Mystery Train* feeling as if the spirit of Elvis can save us. Indeed, it is ineffectual. The spiritual presence of Elvis cannot, in Jarmusch's film, reclaim what is absent.

Strikingly different is the attitude exemplified by the character of Elvis in *True Romance*. In this film, Elvis speaks as a representative of a culture of violence. Nerdy Clarence is set up with a prostitute by his friends, only to find that he has fallen in love with her. The true test of this romance is whether or not Clarence can free himself from the jealousy and rage associated with his knowledge of her past. The spirit of Elvis convinces him that the only way he can be free from these feelings, and the only way that Clarence and Alabama can have a true romance, is if Clarence is willing to confront her pimp with violence. This should come as no surprise, for Clarence has already confessed that for him Elvis was a representative, a harbinger, of recklessness, of rock 'n' roll, of living fast, and of dying young. Elvis is still present with us, you see. He is not absent at all. His death did not take him away but reinforced the point of his life, assured us that his spirit would remain, that 'not givin' a fuck about anything' would become a holy calling. In this film Elvis is not confused about the violence of the world, he is an instigator of it, the original 'bad boy.' Everything the southern preachers said about Elvis and how he would bring about the decline of society turned out to be true.

While this expresses some of the attitude about Elvis and violence as exemplified in the other Elvis Movies we are discussing, *Wild at Heart, 3000 Miles to Graceland,* and *Six-String Samurai,* it does not capture the hopefulness in these films. Granted, *True Romance* does conclude with a happy ending, but one bought at great price. One imagines that there might have been other ways to attain it than the one chosen by the protagonists in that film. In contrast, *Wild at Heart, 3000 Miles to Graceland,* and *Six-String Samurai* paint a more ambiguous picture of the relationship of the spirit of Elvis to the surrounding violence. For, while in *True Romance* Elvis appears to be entirely complicit in the violence, and in *Mystery Train* he appears powerless against it, in these other three films the spirit of Elvis not only lives in the midst of violent lives, but also provides a means of liberation and escape from them.

Though no onscreen apparitions are seen in these three films, the spirit of Elvis provides hope and inspiration. Surely Sailor's violence is a result of the same wild heart shared by Elvis, and it leads him to violence and prison, as it led Elvis in *Jailhouse Rock.* However, this violent element is balanced in Sailor by his love for Lula, a love that will save him from the violence that mars his life. This love, like the violence, is part of the spirit of Elvis. *Love Me Tender,* Sailor sings. This song is the salvation of the characters. The man singing this song is the true Sailor, singing in the true spirit of Elvis.

In *3000 Miles to Graceland* and *Six-String Samurai* the viewer is introduced to the same ambiguity concerning the spirit of Elvis. Impersonators rob a casino and kill all who are in their way. They turn on each other and betray their brothers. Yet, for the central character, the son and heir of Elvis, this violent journey is a quest for peace, a means of escape from that violence. The spirit of Elvis, exemplified by his inheritance of Elvis's boat, named *Graceland,* is what calls him out of his past into a new and redemptive future.

Likewise Buddy's journey to Lost Vegas to claim the throne of the King is a violent pilgrimage, the end of which promises to be a release from constant struggle and war. In these three films, then, while Elvis's spirit is clearly placed within and alongside the violence of society, it is also a promise of salvation. For all the ways that Elvis's life played out wild and uncontrollable, it was also redemptive. For all the ways that his death was tragic, it was also transformative. For all the ways that his absence is present in the violence of daily life, it is also present in moments of love and redemption and hope.

— Ambiguous Angels —

The remaining three Elvis Movies that we have looked at are, for the most part, without this level of violence. Interestingly, they also differ from these other films in their presentation of the absent Elvis Presley. All three of these movies feature Elvis as a living character. *Heartbreak Hotel* is the least successful at this for, while David Keith does look and act a little like Elvis, the illusion is never complete. This effect is unsettling in a way that it is not in *Wild at Heart*, for in that movie Nicolas Cage is not playing Elvis, but rather someone who has some of the characteristics of the King. Consequently, while watching Cage's performance one is constantly reminded of the real Elvis but watching Keith's performance only serves to remind you that this is not Elvis. *Finding Graceland* and *Bubba Ho-tep* avoid these problems by setting their movies in the present day and, therefore, by allowing Keitel and Campbell to play an Elvis twenty years older than at the time of his death. In addition, they both assume that there is some ambiguity regarding the true identity of these characters. Viewers are never quite sure if their stories are real. This ambiguity in regards to their identity, therefore, is a way of confronting the absence of the real Elvis Presley in these films.

Another commonality between these three films is found in their presentation of Elvis as a transformative figure in the lives of other characters. Keitel's Elvis in *Finding Graceland* appears as an angelic presence, a stranger who drops into the lives of individuals to make things right. The film opens with a scene of a truck driver, who has given Elvis a lift, offering his tearful thanks for the way Elvis has helped him face a critical issue in his life. The main plot of the movie shows how Elvis helps a grieving husband overcome his own sense of guilt at his wife's death in an automobile accident, which we discover at the finale also included the truck driver from the opening scene. It seems that Elvis's life, after his faked death, has been filled with this kind of wandering ministry. Elvis is a savior angel who brings redemption and forgiveness to hurting souls. He is Christ on the road to Emmaus, anonymous to his traveling companions, with the face of a stranger, but present and salvific nonetheless.

Likewise, Keith's Elvis in *Heartbreak Hotel* is able to transform the lives of a broken family. By helping them to repair and redecorate their hotel and by enabling the mother to smile and feel young again, Elvis leaves a lasting impression. His presence, like the presence of an angel or a divinity, sets the family back upon the right road and gives them a second chance, like the angelic visitors to Abraham and Lot, who by coming into their homes were able to offer them salvation.

Elvis, the helpful angel is not without ambiguity in these films, however. For while the character of Elvis does change the lives of those he touches, his own life is not without its sorrows. In *Heartbreak Hotel* Elvis is trapped by his fame, grieving for his mother, and watching his career sink ever lower. As much as the family needs his presence, so he needs theirs. He too learns lessons and is transformed by the encounter. He comes to understand the joys of normal life, of working with his hands and living simply. He finds a surrogate family to replace the one that he has lost. He recaptures his lost youth. One almost wants to believe at the end of the film that Elvis did find a way to escape from his tragic life, that he did end up with a family like this one, and that he was young again before he grew old.

Similarly, Harvey Keitel's Elvis is an ambiguous angel, perhaps himself a normal man who assumes the identity of Elvis to hide his own pain. He is terrified of performing on stage. He is deluded into believing that when he returns to Graceland he will be met by family and friends who will welcome him home. The transformative power that he brings to the lives of others seems to come from his own sources of sorrow.

This same sense of ambiguity is found in the Elvis character of *Bubba Ho-tep*, who must overcome his own tragedies in order to defeat the evil presence. Elvis, long trapped in the nursing home, has to find his self-respect and come to terms with his comically convoluted past in order to perform the work of a savior, less an itinerant or domestic angel than an apocalyptic one. Interestingly, while this Elvis must confront the biggest challenge and the greatest evil, while he must do battle with forces of death and destruction, while he struggles, not with broken hearts and shattered dreams, but with a soul-sucking demon, this Elvis is also the most comic and most ironic of them all.

Bruce Campbell, a marvelously ironic actor, embodies Elvis in all of his overweight, side-burned, white-jumpsuited glory and then he amplifies these characteristics in our aging hero. His Elvis wears the mutton chops, but his hair is gray and unkempt. He is out of shape and, because of a broken hip, barely able to walk. When he does take off his bathrobe and put on his white jumpsuit to do battle with the villain, he must do so with the aid of a walker, and later, a motorized wheelchair. The old, fat Elvis of the parodies is here taken to an extreme. Yet, ironically, it is this Elvis who saves the day, who defeats evil, who, like an angel from the Book of Revelation, confronts the powers of death and hell.

— Conclusion —

Popcorn eaten, movies over, I had to sit in stunned silence. For the most part Elvis Movies are not fun, or when they are meant to be fun they are really awful (thank you, *Bubba Hotep*, for being the exception to this rule). They offer ambiguous and violent visions with the absent Elvis ironically present as their central character. This is, I have to say, not the Elvis religion I started out to find. It was supposed to be funny and a little goofy. In these Hollywood movies, however, filled with characters who, if not always southern, are nevertheless white trash, Elvis stands for violence, uncertainty, and loss. Elvis is the apocalyptic messenger. One doesn't seek him out for spiritual advice, but shudders at his presence. When Elvis does appear in these films as an angelic presence, as someone who brings grace to the lives he touches, that presence is never free of ambiguity. The angelic Elvis is himself broken, in need of grace, lost in his own way.

What strikes me about Elvis Movies is not only that they place Elvis in the kinds of religious contexts that I found noticeably absent from both the Graceland and Elvis impersonation phenomena, but that, for the most part, the religious images of Elvis are extremely tragic. Perhaps, however, this is how it must be. After all, Graceland is located in a suburb of Memphis, Whitehaven, whose very name conjures up the racial divide at the heart of America's past and present, and that now threatens to fall to urban decay. After all, Elvis died on his toilet of a massive drug overdose. Ironically, it appears that for Hollywood it is precisely the tragic elements of Elvis Presley's life, death, and legacy that point most clearly to his religious significance. It is as if it is tragedy that makes Elvis holy. This is true, I have found, not only for Elvis's depiction in film, but also for his characterization in fiction.

AN ELVIS FILMOGRAPHY

During the fourteen-year period from 1956 to 1969 Elvis portrayed a singing cowboy (*Love Me Tender*, 20th Century Fox, 1956), an overnight singing sensation (*Loving You*, Paramount, 1957), the aforementioned ex-con (*Jailhouse Rock*, MGM, 1957), a rising New Orleans jazz singer (*King Creole*, Paramount, 1958), a singing GI stationed in Germany (filmed after Elvis's release from the army where he had been 'a singing GI stationed in Germany') (*GI Blues*, Paramount, 1960), a 'half-breed' caught in the middle of a Native American–settler conflict in the old west (*Flaming Star*, 20th Century Fox, 1960), a troubled youth paroled into the custody of his bootlegger uncle (*Wild in the Country*, 20th Century Fox, 1961), a GI returning home to Hawaii (*Blue Hawaii*, Paramount, 1961), the son, and older brother, in a family of Florida homesteaders (*Follow That Dream*, United Artists, 1962), an ex-GI who takes up boxing (*Kid Galahad*, United Artists, 1962), a fishing guide (*Girls, Girls, Girls*, Paramount, 1962), a crop duster who hits on hard times (*It Happened at the World's Fair*, MGM, 1963), a trapeze artist-turned-lifeguard (*Fun in Acapulco*, Paramount, 1963), both a GI and a hillbilly in a rare dual role performance, (*Kissin' Cousins*, MGM, 1964), a racing-car driver (*Viva Las Vegas,* MGM, 1964), a singer-turned-carnival roustabout (*Roustabout,* Paramount, 1964), a night-club singer on vacation (*Girl Happy*, MGM, 1965), a singing rodeo cowboy, (*Tickle Me,* Allied Artists, 1965), a matinee idol touring the Middle East (*Harum Scarum*, MGM, 1965), a riverboat singer with a gambling problem (*Frankie and Johnny*, United Artists, 1966), a helicopter pilot (*Paradise Hawaiian Style*, Paramount, 1966), a singer/racing-car driver (*Spinout*, MGM, 1966), a scuba diver (*Easy Come, Easy Go*, Paramount, 1967), a singer on a tour of Europe (*Double Trouble,* MGM, 1967), an heir to oil money-turned-ski instructor (*Clambake,* United Artists, 1967), a rodeo cowboy (*Stay Away Joe*, MGM, 1968), another racing-car driver (*Speedway*, MGM, 1968), a man who has to work two jobs to pay his rent (*Live a Little Love a Little*, MGM, 1968), an outlaw trying to go straight (*Charro*, National General, 1969), the manager of a 1920s road act (*The Trouble with Girls*, MGM, 1969), and an inner-city doctor (*Change of Habit*, Universal International, 1969).

4

Elvis in Fiction
Memphis Messiah, Jumpsuit Jesus

When I began my quest to identify and understand religious imagery associated with Elvis Presley I was, of course, aware of the existence of Graceland as a tourist attraction to thousands of people every year and of Elvis impersonation as an odd activity on the fringes of culture. I was also somewhat aware that the character of Elvis had been featured in a few films. I was completely shocked, however, to discover that Elvis has such an important place in the world of contemporary literature. Much to my surprise, it seems that Elvis stands among the ranks of recurring literary characters such as James Bond, Sherlock Holmes, Tarzan, and Conan the Barbarian. Like these characters, the character of Elvis has been featured in countless works of fiction. Unlike his companions, however, who ended up trapped in one particular genre or another, the character of Elvis appears in a diverse set of literary genres and has been brought to life, or back to life as it were, by a diverse set of authors. Elvis has made appearances in mystery novels, in science-fiction stories, in historical fiction, and in parodies. The character of Elvis has been featured in novels written by the most sincere and devoted, yet relatively unknown, fans as well as by popular and critically acclaimed authors. Out of all the places that I have found Elvis in my studies, the world of fiction remains the most surprising to me.

As Elvis Novels are quite plentiful and diverse, published by small 'publish on demand' companies as well as by large mainstream houses, and written by Elvis fans as well as well-known literary figures, this chapter will include a general overview of the many different kinds of Elvis literature as a sort of annotated bibliography at the end. The main portion of this chapter, however, will be devoted to an important subset of these novels. The novels chosen for more detailed analysis exhibit two important characteristics that set them apart from the rest. First, these books are among the best-written of the Elvis-themed novels. Second, these books illustrate two important religious paradigms found in much of this literature, the paradigms of the 'Memphis Messiah' and the 'Jumpsuit Jesus.'

— Memphis Messiah —

Some books featuring Elvis as a main character intentionally approach the figure of Elvis from a religious perspective. Bob Laughlin's surprisingly un-funny *The Gospel of Elvis* is an example of religious fiction that addresses its subject in a decidedly tongue-in-cheek fashion. Taking the form and style of a New Testament Gospel, *The Gospel of Elvis* purports to be 'Translated out of the Original Tongues and with former Translations diligently compared and revised.' In this decidedly warped version of the Christian Gospel, an angel, Dizzy Gillespie, appears to Gladys, the mother of Elvis, as Gabriel appeared to the Virgin Mary. The angel prophesied that, among other things, her son would be known as the King of Rock 'n' Roll. (Laughlin 2000: 3: 3–7) At the time of Elvis's birth, angels appeared to shepherds on the outskirts of Tupelo to inform them that 'unto you is born this day in the city of Jethro a Savior, which is the Messiah and the Lord.' (4: 1–6) Later, when an adult Elvis is led, like Jesus, into the wilderness to be tempted by the devil, he resists the enticement of Satan to make bread from stones by saying, 'It is written that man shall not live by bread alone, but also by peanut butter and 'nanas and bacon and twinkies and . . .' (11: 1–4).

Such nonsense continues through eighty-eight chapters and includes references to the Beatles, Clarence Thomas and Anita Hill, and Oral Roberts. It ends, as the lives of Jesus and the real Elvis did, with a tragic betrayal and death, followed by a resurrection.

> And it came to pass that much others claimed to have seen Elvis. Much verily swore that the Lord was variously working as a short order cook, a pump jockey at a fillin' station, and a lumberjack in the East. It got so thou couldnst watch a ballgame on tv without seeing Elvis in the stands, though it came to light that these were Elvis impersonators, or as they like to call themselves, the first priests of the Roman Elvic Church. 'Twas even said that one day, Elvis's face appeared on a tortilla down in Mexico . . . (88: 7–10)

Continuing in the mold of ironic religious visions of Elvis is Steve Werner's *Elvis and the Apocalypse*, in which ancient manuscripts reveal the truth about the life of Elvis Presley, and *Templars of the Christian Brotherhood* by David Paul and Geoffrey Todd, which reveals that the TCB is engaged in battle with the evil forces of 'Helter Skelter.'

Exemplifying a more serious approach in religious Elvis Novels are *Clothed in Light* by Paul Jaffe and *Elvis A. Eagle: A Magical Adventure* by Carl R. Sinclair. In the first of these the author tells Elvis's story from a first-person perspective beginning with his death and transformation, a feat made possible for the author by a kind of spiritual channeling. In *Elvis A. Eagle* the character of Elvis is allegorized as an eagle whose role it is to reveal the eagle in all of us. These books, however, are all rather lightweight, and finally, uninteresting. This is not the end of the subject when it comes to religious characterizations of Elvis in fiction, however.

Elvis and Nixon

One of the most interesting fictional examinations of Elvis's own religious self-understanding is found in the historical novel *Elvis and Nixon* by Jonathan Lowy. This novel takes as its setting the infamous meeting between Elvis and President Richard Nixon in 1970. Against that backdrop, and an exploration of the motives Elvis might have had for initiating such a visit, Lowy explores the messianic pretensions of his character, a small-town boy from Tupelo who dared to attempt, and achieved, a meeting with the most powerful man in the world.

Elvis's strange journey begins at Graceland where, heavily drugged and ill, he is surrounded by family and friends who need, and use, him as a source of money. Lowy describes Elvis's perception of the situation in terms that evoke both Yahweh's repentance before the flood and Jesus' frustration with the people of Nazareth. Elvis has created these people, made them who they are by his money and fame, but also by his talent, power, and grace. Unfortunately, while Elvis perceived himself as evolving and while he was witnessing the growth of a new faith centered on his personality and life, the people around him were only interested in money. They had lost faith in him and so, within the walls of his own house, he was, like Jesus in his home town of Nazareth, impotent.

Making a break from the faithless family at Graceland, Elvis takes to the road. His thoughts lead him to a comparison of himself with Jesus. With Christmas only a week away, Elvis wonders why he should even consider that to be important. Now that he had come to understand himself as a master in the same sense as Jesus, why should the birth of an equal be of interest to him? Later, in a conversation with an FBI agent, Elvis makes his religious self-understanding public in an attempt to prove that he should be issued an official FBI badge and made a special drug enforcement officer. His argument is based on his ability to heal those who are addicted to drugs, including heroin.

> 'I'm in Las Vegas the other month, after a show' – Elvis stood up now and began to walk quickly around the room – 'and I get to talking with this comic, Ernie Charles, fast-talking Jewish guy in the Green Room, trying jokes when he breaks into tears all the sudden. Well I talk to him and he tells me "Elvis, it's the drugs," heroin, he's shaking and crying, telling me he needs a fix bad but he don't have the money could I loan him some. So I walk over to him, and I place one hand on his forehead and the other around his arm. "Show me the marks," I say to him, "where you shot this shit into your veins." And he does, on both arms, and I lay hands on 'em. And I'm thinking all the while, and saying aloud – a feelin' comes over me – "Devils leave this man, leave him and he shall goeth in the path of righteousness, shall liveth in the straight and narrow way, praise be, and the rest." Then I remove my hands for a minute, and I cover his mouth then his ears then his eyes, and then I slap him hard on the forehead. And all the sudden, he stops shaking, stops crying, stops sweating. And he says "I'm cured. Elvis, I'm cured." . . . And he was, was the thing. Never touched the stuff since. I done this a few times now.' (Lowy 2001: 267)

Elvis and Nixon offers a critically ironic look at Elvis as a messianic figure. Clearly, Lowy, by offering a fictional account of Elvis's self-image, demonstrates the irony inherent in any proclamation of Elvis's divinity. One might understand how Elvis, broken, addicted to prescription drugs, and seemingly infinitely wealthy and powerful, might come to see himself in messianic terms. From a small cabin in Tupelo to a mansion in Memphis, from a nobody to a man who was entertained by presidents, surely, this man must be the Son of God. But, Lowy's narrative implies, it is much harder to understand how anyone else would make a god out of this man.

That's Alright Mama

Gerald Duff likewise struggles with the ambiguous legacy of Elvis in his novel *That's Alright Mama*. Adopting the convention of publishing a 'found manuscript' written by the secret twin of Elvis, this novel tells the story of Elvis, from birth to death, from the perspective of his twin brother Jesse, declared dead at birth but secretly passed off to members of the Presley extended family. The story begins with Jesse's recounting of his father's description of the night of the twins' conception, an account that assigns a messianic sense to the twin births. Gladys, the boys' mother, experiences a vision in the moon. She knew from that moment that she would have twins, but was obsessed by the knowledge that, though there would be two of them, there would be only one soul between them. Two bodies, two forms, but only one person.

At the prompting of another vision Gladys moves the family to Memphis, with Jesse tagging along as Elvis's cousin. In Memphis the visions continue and the sense of messianic destiny spawned by Gladys takes hold of Elvis himself. Just before his death, he confesses his belief about his destiny to Jesse. Elvis, he tells Jesse, has come to understand that, like Jesus, he has been put upon the Earth for a divine purpose. His fate has been revealed to him in the pages of esoteric books about religion and mysticism and by private visions and revelations.

> 'Jesus,' I said again, but this time I wasn't trying to call up his name like the answer to a riddle. I said it in the

same way you would if you'd just seen a big wreck on the highway or watched the windows in your house bust out from a bomb going off in the neighborhood. You know what I mean. Slow, and every part of the name long and drawn out.

'It's pyramids in South America,' said Elvis. 'In Peru and all down in there. They got these drawings on the wall of a man singing to a bunch of people, to a whole society and a whole civilization. These little markings are called hieroglyphics, Jesse, cut into them rocks by these priests. It's signs to people that know how to read them.' (Duff 1995: 257)

This belief in messianic destiny is profoundly at odds with the appearance of Elvis in the eyes of his brother. His body was covered with sweat. When he lifts his shirt to wipe the sweat from his face, Jesse sees that sweat is standing in the folds of fat on his gigantic white belly.

As in *Elvis and Nixon*, *That's Alright Mama* shows the contrast between the messianic grandeur of Elvis and the brutal reality of his drug abuse. Indeed, as the novel unfolds it is revealed that at crucial moments in Elvis's life, including the first recordings at Sun Studios and the Comeback Special, it is Jesse, not Elvis, who is performing. Time and again Jesse stands in for his brother, even making love to Priscilla in the guise of Elvis and, by doing so, holding the marriage together. The twin brothers are two aspects of a single life. One, Elvis, is a messianic figure crucified by his drug abuse. The other, Jesse, is an invisible partner, free from most of Elvis's tragic habits, but also free of his destiny.

Both *That's Alright Mama* and *Elvis and Nixon* are novels that pursue the question of the messianic sense of destiny of Elvis himself. They both place the character of Elvis against backdrops that fuel his own sense of grandeur. For Lowy, this backdrop is the group of Memphis friends, family members, and business associates who clung to Elvis for financial support as he lifted them all out of southern poverty. Their position demanded that they prop up his sense of self-importance to help him maintain the persona that brought in money and fame. It also demanded that they serve as disciples and unwavering supporters, agreeing with his every word and idea. The messianic image thus created stood in sharp contrast to the reality of Elvis's drug use, and his declining health, declining talent, and declining fame. Indeed, the one may well have served as the cause for the other. For Duff, this backdrop is the religio-cultural predispositions of Elvis's mother, Gladys. Because Gladys saw the world in terms of fundamentalist Christianity and ignorant superstitions, Elvis was destined to do the same. Again, the belief in messianic destiny is in contrast to the reality of Elvis's tragic later life. Perhaps it can be said that, for Duff's Elvis character, messianic visions served as a self-refuting prophecy. There was no way that a boy from Tupelo, raised ignorant and superstitious, could ever be the messiah, even if he moved to a mansion in Memphis.

'Nothing good can come from Nazareth' was an insult thrown at Jesus in reference to the backwardness of his home town. The same perhaps applies to Elvis as envisioned by the two authors in question, and perhaps explains something of the ambiguous and ironic place of Elvis in pop culture in general. 'Nothing good could come from Memphis.' This Memphis Messiah may have the characteristics of a savior, of a messiah, his life may be filled with success and accomplishment and dignity and charity, but this messiah is also from Memphis. He is a country boy out of his league, a red-neck who can't handle success, a pretender to a place in American high-class society. He is just a Memphis Messiah.

— Jumpsuit Jesus —

Another interesting and recurring approach to the religious significance of Elvis Presley is found in a set of novels that have as a central character an Elvis impersonator. These novels, *Graceland* by Chris Abani, *Me, the Moon, and Elvis Presley* by Christopher Hope, *Stark Raving Elvis* by William McCranor Henderson, and *Biggest Elvis* by P. F. Kluge, are all stories that place Elvis impersonators in the position of a sacrificial savior, or – considering that the impersonators' acts of sacrificial atonement take place while robed in the traditional white jumpsuit of Elvis in the Vegas years – of a Jumpsuit Jesus.

Graceland

Abani's *Graceland* is set in the urban context of Lagos, Nigeria and follows the exploits of a teenage boy by the name of Elvis. In the midst of urban blight and squalor, Lagos is a city that shows signs of the ubiquity of American culture and in which the image of Elvis Presley serves as a sign of hope and freedom. Elvis attempts to make his living by impersonating this image of American splendor, a career that leads him to more profitable work as a private escort for wealthy women and finally as a drug trafficker. In one passage Elvis's performance of 'Hound Dog' for tourists lounging beside a hotel swimming pool is described. His wig is on backwards, his accent so thick the tourists cannot understand what he is saying. They are not even certain that he is doing an Elvis impersonation. When they ask what he wants, he speaks clearly, however. He wants money.

In a complex plot-line that can only be hinted at here, but which should be appreciated for its reverential parody of the lives of both Elvis Presley and Jesus Christ, Elvis falls foul of a local military leader called 'de Colonel' and is left for dead. Meanwhile, his friend Redemption also runs into trouble with the military leader and, like Jesus' family fleeing from Herod, is forced to flee the country, only returning when he hears, again like Jesus, that the Colonel has been killed. The Colonel's assassin is another friend of Elvis, by the name of the Beggar King, or de King, who leads a failed rebellion against the military forces, which results in the mass slaughter of many residents of the city, including Elvis's father. In the process, the King himself is killed. Much to Elvis's surprise, Redemption offers him his passport and, after much discussion, Elvis agrees to take it in order to go to America. He is the one, out of all of them, it seems, who has a chance to survive there, and who, because of his intelligence, has a chance to thrive. "'Okay, Elvis done leave de country,' Redemption announced with a laugh' (Abani 2004: 318).

Elvis, the Elvis impersonator, is a kind of savior for his people, for the down-and-out and suffering people of Lagos. The salvation he offers comes in the form of his own escape from Lagos to America. The salvation event is a communal accomplishment, requiring that de King give up his life and that Redemption give up his own chance to escape, as well as requiring not only that Elvis lose his father, but that he lose his dignity by dressing as that other Elvis, begging for money from strangers while wearing his wig 'front to back.' The salvation is also communal in that Elvis, by escaping to America, continues to offer hope to those he leaves behind. His escape is a promise of their salvation.

Me, the Moon, and Elvis Presley

Another impersonator novel set in Africa is Christopher Hope's *Me, the Moon, and Elvis Presley*. This novel moves back and forth between the childhood of a little girl in the town of Lutherburg sold into slavery for six bars of soap and her adult life as deputy mayor of the same South

African town. In her childhood in the 1950s, Mimi was exposed to the music of Elvis Presley as it was experienced by the locals, verging on a religious cult. The town's devotion to Elvis was so pronounced that other local communities saw fit to condemn it as idolatry. The village of Abraham's Grave accused them of offering adoration to idols of the temple of Baal. This criticism only strengthened the resolve of the community in their Elvis devotion, however. Someone took the stones used to spell out the town's name on a local hillside and rearranged them in the form of a huge effigy of Elvis.

Like any religious movement, this one split into competing sects. Some in town claimed that salvation was through works, others by faith alone. Some claimed that the pilgrimage to Memphis would be necessary in order to one day see the King face to face. Others believed that patient faith would be rewarded and that Elvis would one day come to live among the people.

Though this infatuation with Elvis gradually passed from the community, it would play a key role in Mimi's later life when a character named Pascal comes to Lutherburg and opens what turns out to be an interracial bar and night-club, the first of its sort in the town and something that results in controversy before the spirit of the endeavor catches on. In the book's finale, Pascal and Mimi work together to organize a community tribute to Elvis as a tourist attraction for the town. The event includes an Elvis impersonator contest, which Pascal has rigged so that he can claim the cash prize and the free trip to Graceland. To everyone's surprise, Pascal wobbles onto the stage in an Elvis jumpsuit. Rigged or not, however, Pascal is clearly the winner. He is the latter-day King with satin jumpsuit, high collar, a gold medallion, and rolls upon rolls of fat. He is a winner, not only in terms of authenticity and sheer rock 'n' roll genius, but also in terms of the peace, love, and reconciliation that he brought to the community.

Elvis religion

In *Me, the Moon, and Elvis Presley*, Pascal as Elvis impersonator offers redemptive transformation to a South African community that has progressed beyond its past of institutionalized apartheid but which is still divided along racial lines. As Elvis had bridged the distance between the races in the 1950s, with his mixture of African-American blues and Appalachian country, and as his recordings had done so in this African town by originating a kind of cult that crossed all barriers of race, gender, and class, so now Pascal, Elvis returned and incarnate, offers redemption. Those who prophesied Elvis's coming had been right. Elvis did come to Lutherburg. But he came short and fat and round in a stark white jumpsuit looking less like a star and more like the moon. He is not a rock star but a common con artist. Yet, his revealed status as a con man does not alter the truth that he brings to Lutherburg. Indeed, it is the wink in the eye of this Elvis that makes his redemptive act possible. His escape with the prize money and the all-expenses-paid trip to Graceland are seen as a fitting ascension for this Jumpsuit Jesus. Even when they come to know more about his history of con tricks and deceptions, the townspeople cannot give up the hope that he has made it to Graceland.

> Maybe he was that very day sitting in Graceland?
> Was it as big as the pictures? And did it have long white columns out front? And pink satin sofas and a black bedroom suite with white leather trim? Was Pascal looking over the King's eight-foot bed and genuine milk-bar right inside the house where the King sat around drinking shakes? The more they talked the clearer it became that they could have sent no one better to Memphis than Pascal Le Gros who, after all, looked a bit like Colonel Tom Parker, didn't he? He was sassy and streetwise and smart; whatever those damn Yanks threw at him, the fat man could handle. Yes, they were happy he was in Graceland. (Hope 1997: 262)

Biggest Elvis

Set in a Philippines night-club called Graceland, P. F. Kluge's *Biggest Elvis* is the story of a trio of impersonators: Baby Elvis, who performs the material from Elvis's early years; Dude Elvis, who performs as the Elvis of the movie years; and Biggest Elvis, who performs as Elvis in all of his Vegas jumpsuit glory. Wade Wiggins, who as Biggest Elvis is at the core of the novel, describes his performances as religious experiences, revelatory not only for himself, but for his audience as well. His performances are sacrificial acts. While the Navy guys in the audience might not have understood him, surely the local girls, raised in the land of relics and icons and saints and martyrs, raised in the land of passion plays, surely they would see his act for what it was. This was Elvis, come again, not a comeback special, but a second coming. To the strains of Richard Strauss he steps on stage and the message he sends is clear, 'here is my body, bloated for you' (Kluge 1996: 11–12).

Indeed, Biggest Elvis is so enraptured by the salvific aspects of his performance that he confides in, or boasts to, a local priest about the spiritual power channeled through him. The priest, encouraged by Biggest Elvis to see for himself, attends a performance at Graceland. Though he finds the claims of Biggest Elvis to be blasphemous, he also finds them intriguing. He had always said that if Christ were to return to the world, he would surely come first to Olongapo, surely he would come to the worst place. And that was precisely what Wade Wiggins had told him about Elvis.

After the performance, Biggest Elvis tries to drive his point home to the priest. The comparison between the work of the two men is just too much to ignore. Both priest and impersonator work for dead men who refuse to stay dead. They both inspire shrines, music, visions, miracles, rituals, and belief in resurrection. Following this conversation, the priest is so concerned about competition from Biggest Elvis that he burns Wiggins's house to the ground as a threat. If he was to be Judas, he thinks, then he would play the part fully. The following passage offers a glimpse into the arsonist's motivation.

> The shrine, the relics, the half-holy music, the incarnation and reincarnation, death and return, absolutely fraudulent and utterly convincing, it was happening here and fast, so that its triumph seemed shockingly easy and years from now I might look back and say, of course, I should have known, it was all so perfect, where else but here, who else but him. Him. The god of Graceland. (106–107)

The true salvation achieved by Biggest Elvis is not revealed until many years later when Wade Wiggins finds himself as an observer of a confrontation between Filipinos and the American Army. Just at the moment when violence is about to erupt, Wiggins, Biggest Elvis, steps between the two opposing camps and begins to sing. Without really thinking about what he was going to do or say, or what the outcome of his actions might be, he stepped into the war zone between two angry camps and thinks to himself, 'Resurrecting Elvis never felt more right. Where else but here? Who else but me? Second chance for Elvis, second chance for me. Second chance for the audience' (326). Someone throws bottles at him from a car window and he is able to avoid them only by recalling his stage moves, those hokey karate chops and kicks of Elvis at his fattest. But, he understands, he cannot escape them all. This is a fate he is willing to embrace. 'Elvis as willing, easy, target. This is my body, assholes, broken for you' (327). Biggest Elvis, a would-be Jesus in a jumpsuit, receives the anger and blows intended for others. The conflict is diffused, all of the violence meant for the Filipinos is heaped upon Elvis. Unlike Jesus or Elvis, Biggest Elvis lives, but like them his body is broken and bloody. Biggest Elvis performs the work of a martyred saint, a suffering servant. As he channels Elvis, he channels Jesus, and, like the characters in the other two novels we have discussed, he brings salvation to a people much in need.

Stark Raving Elvis

Stark Raving Elvis by William McCranor Henderson continues the theme of the Elvis impersonator as a salvific figure. This is the story of Prince Byron, an Elvis fan who, after meeting Elvis and being given a gun by the King, becomes convinced that he is destined to complete the King's ministry, much as Jesus completed the work of John the Baptist. Elvis confides to him that he is too far gone to continue and that it will be up to Byron to carry on. The King called Prince Byron to carry out his mission and then, to seal the deal, gave him his gun. Byron's belief in his own destiny is so great that even his dreams reveal the truth of Elvis's revelation. In his dreams he find Elvis in a coffin, his heart on a plate next to him, sizzling, like a steak. Byron douses it with A-1 Steak Sauce and does the only thing he can do, puts it in his mouth and begins to chew.

After the death of Elvis, Byron pursues his dream with even more single-mindedness, moving to Las Vegas to make his break as Elvis's successor. Convinced at first that his calling is to perform as the early Elvis, without jumpsuit, he nevertheless gives in to the pressure of expectations and dresses in a jumpsuit. The power of the suit is that of a totem for him as it surely will be a sacramental vessel for those in his audience. Visions of the jumpsuit haunted him.

> He knew it could never be a simple matter; the jumpsuit wasn't just a costume. There were sinister possibilities – Elvis had fattened in it, putrefied and died. There was danger attached to it.

> But where there's danger, Byron realized, there's also power, and he had come to recognize that late Elvis was full of the most majestic sort of power. (Henderson 1984: 149–150)

As Elvis was corrupted by the power of the jumpsuit, so is Byron, however, turning to drugs and alcohol, and betraying the woman who has stood beside him throughout. As time passes, the distinction between reality and dream becomes completely blurred for Byron. He is King Byron. He is Elvis. His journey into madness concludes at a Las Vegas impersonator contest at which, though he is the crowd's favorite, he loses to another impersonator. Using the gun given to him by Elvis he kidnaps the other contestants and the promoters. At the demands of the crowd, who do not know of his crime, however, he is returned to the stage and pronounced the victor. His prize is a brilliant white jumpsuit worn by Elvis himself. The victory is shocking, however, for the people are not cheering for Byron, but for Elvis. In a moment of madness he rips the suit from his body, stands naked before the crowd, and hurls the costume into the waiting hands below him. The result is a riot that destroys the suit and bloodies the audience. Its result is also a moment of clarity for Byron, a moment of sanity.

> Byron saw the riot unfold out of the corner of his eye. It didn't concern him now. His role was played out. He floated above it all, over it, free of it. He felt light and perfect, naked like a baby with no name, no past. He was brand new. (261)

For Byron, to wear the jumpsuit was to take on the mantle of Elvis and, like Elvis, it meant that his life would be lost to the demands of those around him. Like Elvis, Byron gave everything to those who were fans, to those who needed whatever brand of salvation he was able to give.

Like Elvis, like a Jumpsuit Jesus, he gives his all to the crowd. Unlike Elvis and unlike Jesus, however, Byron is able to save his life, and perhaps reclaim his sanity.

In all of these novels a central Christ-like character, in the guise of Elvis, takes upon himself the dreams and aspirations of those around him and sacrifices himself for the salvation of others. In *Graceland* the suffering of Elvis, and indeed of his family and nation, is transformed into hope and promise when Elvis is given the chance to leave Africa for America. Elvis is sent as a representative, with someone else's passport, because it is believed that he can best represent the dreams of his people. Likewise in *Me, the Moon, and Elvis Presley*, Pascal takes the hopes of Lutherburg with him to Graceland. Even when the people discover his crimes, discover his sins against them, they remain convinced that he was the right man for the journey to the promised land. It is almost as if Pascal, by the commission of his sins and crimes, is made worthy of the honor bestowed upon him. It is Pascal the con man who redeems the community by integrating the bar, and it is Pascal the con man who is the incarnation of the promised coming of King Elvis.

In *Biggest Elvis*, Wade Wiggins offers the people of the Graceland night-club a bit of the holy presence of Elvis, but, unlike Baby Elvis and Dude Elvis, he can only do this through the destruction of his own body. It is only by making himself overweight and sickly that he is able to channel the power of Elvis and perform 'American Trilogy'. He is to this group of people both a priest and a savior, both a mediator of the presence of Elvis and the very incarnation of that presence. His final mediation, when he stands between the soldiers and his friends is the ultimate act of sacrifice. It is this same sacrifice that Byron is called upon to make in *Stark Raving Elvis*. In order to mediate the salvific presence of Elvis to the masses he must dress in the white jumpsuit, he must abuse drugs, he must be unfaithful to his lover, and he must let himself deteriorate both physically and mentally. It is through this suffering, and this suffering alone, that salvation can come.

This is a common theme throughout these novels. It is not, after all, the young and virile Elvis who brings salvation, it is the overweight, jumpsuited Elvis. The jumpsuit, the drugs, the weight, the depression, these are the stripes by which we are healed. This is what makes Elvis the god into Elvis the man. This is his incarnation, where he takes on the fleshiness of his fans and in so doing makes himself one of us and thus able to save us.

— Conclusion —

Well, there you have it. Memphis Messiah and Jumpsuit Jesus. If you're looking for a religious Elvis you will find him in the pages of contemporary literature, a drug-addled rock star convinced of his own messianic destiny, an impersonator in a post-colonial setting offering salvation to the lost. Again, this is not Saint Elvis as I was looking for him. This Saint Elvis isn't all that fun. As a matter of fact, I don't know how anyone could worship this King. He is deluded by drugs into believing in his own messianic destiny. He is such a product of superstitious and fundamentalist religion that it haunts him to his grave. He is overweight. He is dishonest. He is at his wits' end, the end of the road, about to go off the deep end. He looks little like the picture on a postage stamp and a lot like you and me. Yet this is the Elvis that comes to save us, flickering on movie screens and rising from the pages of a book. Saint Elvis, Memphis Messiah, Jumpsuit Jesus.

This Elvis thing is turning into more than I bargained for. I set out to find out if my own late-night, emergency room, Memphis encounter with Elvis faith was an aberration or a trend, if Elvis really was worshipped and revered. I don't know what I expected to find at Graceland and at Elvis impersonator competitions, probably nothing more than a few very deluded nuts, and certainly not the fun-loving, mostly sensible fans and collectors that I did encounter. But I know that I didn't expect to find this, this ambiguous angel offering violent visions, this Memphis Messiah and Jumpsuit Jesus. This isn't just a saint for men in white jumpsuits or mourners at Elvis's grave. This is a savior for our own violent, ironic, media dominated, junk food age. This is a saint we all should be able to identify as a whole.

Graceland and Vegas did not provide much in the way of Elvis religion, but film and fiction are another story. It doesn't seem to matter whether or not there is a growing cult devoted to Elvis Presley or whether impersonators act as a sacred priesthood. Popular culture seems to have found what even his most devoted fans have not seen, religious meaning deeply present in the character of Elvis Presley. If this is true in terms of movies and novels, what about other areas of culture and entertainment, what about the thing that first gave the world Elvis Presley, what about Elvis in popular music?

AN ELVIS BIBLIOGRAPHY

Historical Fiction

Many novels about the King approach their subject through fictionalizing historical events. One of the earliest books to include Elvis as a central figure, through a thinly veiled pseudonym for the character, was Gail Brewer-Giorgio's *Orion: The Living Superstar of Song* (1979. New York, Pocket

Books). *Orion* tells the story of rock-and-roll star Orion in a fashion that borrows heavily from the life of Elvis Presley. Its importance, other than being one of the first Elvis Novels, is found in the fact that it includes a plot twist involving Orion faking his own death, a theme that recurs in many Elvis Novels, and in the fact that it was written by a woman who was instrumental in perpetuating the theory that the real Elvis Presley had done just that. This convention of fictionalizing the life of Elvis Presley under a false name is also employed by Mark Childress in 1990's *Tender* (New York, Ballantine), the story of a rock star from East Tupelo, Mississippi by the name of Leroy Kirby. In a more direct manner, William F. Buckley Jr.'s *Elvis in the Morning* (2001. New York, Harcourt) tells the story of Elvis Presley and his relationship with the fictional Orson, a young Elvis fan and close acquaintance of Priscilla, who befriends Elvis while the star is stationed in Germany and who remains close to him throughout his life. Samuel Charters takes a different approach in *Elvis Presley Calls his Mother after the Ed Sullivan Show* (1992. Minneapolis, Coffee House Press). This novel is a fictionalized record of Elvis's half of a telephone call to his mother following his famed television appearance.

Fan Fiction

Other novels focus on the impact of the life of Elvis Presley on Elvis fans and society as a whole. Elvis's life figures in Kathryn Stern's *Another Song about the King* (2000. New York, Ballantine) as a backdrop for a story about the relationship between a mother and daughter. In this novel Silvie is told by her mother that she is named for Elvis (her mother claims that 'Silvie' is, loosely speaking, 'Elvis' spelled backwards). Silvie struggles to discover whether her mother's stories of dating Elvis as a teenager are true. More importantly, she struggles to understand the significance of her mother's devotion to the King. Likewise, Elvis fans are at the center of Lenore Vinyard Bechtel's *Thank You, Elvis* (2003. Baltimore, Publish America). This romantic comedy follows the exploits of characters known as 'Presley,' who was born during Elvis's comeback special, and 'Vegas,' born in Las Vegas during an Elvis performance, as they find romance despite their Elvis-fan parents' insistence that they were made for each other. Other novels that we might include in this category are *Lamar's Rebellion* by James S. Gibons (2000. Philadelphia, Xlibris), *Elvis Unplugged* by Marlis Wesseler (1998. London, Oberon), *Graced Land* by Laura Kalpakian (1992. Portland, OR, Blue Heron), and *Elvis Over England* by Barry Hines (1999. New York, Penguin). An important subgenre of Elvis Fan Fiction is made up of those novels that feature Elvis impersonators. These include *My Road Trip to the Pretty Girl Capital of the World* by Brian Yansky (2003. Chicago, Cricket) and *Zip Six* by Jack Gantos (1996. Boulder, CO, Bridge Works).

Speculative Fiction

Speculative fiction is a category of Elvis Novels that either speculates about what might have happened if Elvis had not died or if other events in his life had turned out differently or that speculates on a grander scale about the implications of Elvis. The theme of Elvis faking his own death has already been mentioned as an important element of the conclusion of the novel *Orion*. It is the starting point for the story line in other novels, however. These include *Jesse* by Brian Devall (2003. San Diego, CA, Aventine), and *Wings on a Guitar: August 16, 1977 – If Elvis Hadn't Died!* by Glenda Ivey (2002. Hampton, GA, Southern Charm), as well as *Elvis: The Novel* by Robert Graham and Keith Baty (1984. London, The Do Not Press) in which an alternate life of Elvis is recounted for laughs. Mark McGinty's *Elvis and the Blue Moon Conspiracy* (2003. Edina, MI, Beaver's Pond

Press), which ends up neither as funny as it thinks it is nor as it could have been, tells the story of how Nixon and NASA secretly planned to send Elvis to the moon in Apollo 11 to ensure that the moon landing was even more of an international and historical event than it was otherwise guaranteed to be. Speculative fiction about Elvis may also take the form of science fiction. *Return to Sender* by Les and Sue Fox (1996. Tequesta, FL, West Highland Publishing Company) tells the story of how Elvis spent a fortune to father a son through cutting-edge cloning techniques and place him anonymously with a normal, healthy family. The novel follows the quest of his son Jaime to discover his true birthright. The science-fiction element is even more pronounced in *Elvis Live at Five* by John Paxson (2002. New York, St. Martin's Press), in which a television producer creates a computer-generated Elvis to deliver the nightly news. Finally, Jack Womack's brilliant *Elvissey* (1993. New York, Grove Press) tells the story of travelers from the future who kidnap a 1950s Elvis from an alternate universe in order to take him back to the future to gain control over an Elvis cult.

Mysteries

Fiction associated with Elvis takes a turn into the genre of murder mystery in the work of Daniel Klein. Klein's novels, including *Kill Me Tender* (2002), *Viva Las Vengeance* (2003), *Such Vicious Minds* (2004), and *Blue Suede Clues* (2003) (New York, St. Martin's Minotaur), are all billed as 'a murder mystery featuring the singing sleuth Elvis Presley' and feature the King of Rock and Roll tracking down murderers and solving crimes from his base at Graceland. Something similar is attempted, or at least promised, in Richard D. Weber's *Elvis and Me: A King of Rock Mystery* (2003. Beverly Hills, Alchemy Press). Though Elvis Presley does make a brief appearance in this novel to karate-chop some evil Ku

Klux Klansmen, the Elvis of the title seems to be the name of a dog who accompanies twelve-year-old Robbie Donner on most of his 1964 adventures. Other mysteries that feature Elvis include Kinky Friedman's *Elvis, Jesus, and Coca Cola* (1993. New York, Simon and Schuster), in which the wise-cracking sleuth investigates a mystery surrounding a documentary about Elvis impersonators, and Anne George's *Murder Boogies with Elvis: A Southern Sisters Mystery* (2003. New York, Avon), in which the detective sisters investigate the death of an Elvis impersonator. Other Elvis mysteries include *Mystery of the Missing Elvis* by Elizabeth Levy (2003. New York, Aladdin), *The Elvis and Marilyn Affair* by Robert S. Levinson (1999. New York, Forge), *Elvis in Aspic* by Gordon DeMarch (1999. Portland, OR, Blue Heron), *Elvis Saves* by Bill Yancey (1988. Philadelphia, Xlibris), *Elvis is Alive* by Robert Mickey Maughon (1999. Kodak, TN, Cinnamon Moon), *Shooting Elvis* by Robert Eversz (1997. New York, Grove Press), *The King is Dead* by Sarah Shankman (1992. New York, Pocket Star), and *The Elvis Murders* by Art Bourgeau (1985. New York, Ace).

5

Elvis in Song
Graceland Gospel, Elvis Elegies,
and Ironic Invitationals

Before the *Ed Sullivan Show*, before the dance moves, before the hair and the movies, before Las Vegas and jump-suits, before Graceland, before impersonators, Elvis was about music. The music was, at times, great. His 1954 Sun Studios recordings mark the very beginning of rock 'n' roll. You can hear, in those sessions, the birth of something new as rhythm and blues meets country music, as white meets black, as urban Memphis meets rural Mississippi. Add the strange echo produced by the acoustics of the room, add Elvis, and you have rock 'n' roll. In the opening notes of 'That's Alright Mama' the listener is fooled into expecting a country recording. Indeed, without Elvis it is country. With Elvis it is rock 'n' roll. Even a song that could have been crooned, a song without a driving beat, becomes, for Elvis, a new and exciting thing. 'Blue Moon' defies classification. The minimalist music and the simple lyrics are trans-formed into something new, something haunting, by Elvis and by Elvis alone. 'Just Because', 'Good Rockin' Tonight', 'Milkcow Blues Boogie', 'Baby Let's Play House', and, of course, the near perfect 'Mystery Train': this is Elvis. This is rock and roll.

Of course, the music went beyond 1954 and beyond Sun Studios, but in that year and in that place the floodgates were opened and the world of music would never be the same. Soon after, in 1956 alone, Elvis would release 'Heartbreak Hotel', 'My Baby Left Me', 'Blue Suede Shoes', 'So Glad You're Mine', 'Tutti Frutti', 'One-Sided Love Affair', 'Love Me', 'Anyplace is Paradise', 'Paralyzed', 'Ready Teddy', 'Too Much', 'Hound Dog', 'Anyway You Want Me (That's How I Will Be)', 'Don't Be Cruel', 'Lawdy Miss Clawdy', 'Shake, Rattle and Roll', 'I Want You, I Need You, I Love You', 'Rip It Up', 'I Got a Woman', 'I Was the One', and 'Money Honey'. Many of these songs are only great songs, many of them only rock 'n' roll, because they were recorded by Elvis Presley. Though there certainly were bad songs recorded in his career, many of those written and recorded for his movies, Elvis's music has been profoundly influential in the fifty years since he first recorded at Sun.

Elvis was not all rock and roll, however. His 1966 gospel album, *How Great Thou Art*, went double platinum and earned a Grammy. Elvis's gospel recordings remain favorites among his fans and are often cited by fans as evidence of Elvis's deeply spiritual nature. His recording of Richard Howard's 'I Believe in the Man in the Sky' is regarded by many as a personal confession of faith that simultaneously captures the tragedy of Elvis's life and death. Likewise, Elvis recorded Tommy Dorsey's 'Take My Hand, Precious Lord'. To many fans today, in the wake of Elvis's death, the words of this song sound especially reassuring, and indicate that Elvis's faith in the face of death was secure. Surely, a man who could sing so passionately about his faith in God must have been singing from his heart. R. Goodman's 'Who Am I?' is thought by many fans to be a sign of Elvis's spiritual humility. In this song it is Jesus, not Elvis, who is the King, and it is Jesus who bled and died for a world full of people, including Elvis, who do not deserve such grace.

There is reason to believe that Elvis did take lyrics such as these with the utmost seriousness and by all accounts

Elvis possessed a great appreciation for gospel music. He recorded over three hundred songs with The Jordanaires, a gospel quartet, and toured with J. D. Sumner and the Stamps Quartet throughout the 1970s. Not surprisingly, therefore, his gospel recordings and his Christian faith figure in at least two songs written about Elvis. Merle Haggard's 'From Graceland to the Promised Land' (1977. *My Farewell to Elvis*, MCA) is a tribute to Elvis's religious faith, and is itself an echo of the lyrics to Elvis's gospel songs. According to Haggard, Elvis kept his faith in Jesus until the end of his life when he was taken from his Memphis home to his heavenly mansion. It is also Elvis's gospel recordings that Warren Zevon sings about in 'Jesus Mentioned' (1982. *The Envoy*, Asylum), though with a decidedly ironic twist. Zevon's narrator is going to Memphis, to Graceland, and along the way is thinking of the heavenly mansions, mentioned by Jesus, and sung about by Elvis. He imagines, upon arriving at Graceland, unearthing the King and pleading with him to sing about them one more time.

These two Elvis Songs are just the tip of the iceberg when it comes to songs written about Elvis. It would be a stretch to say that Elvis has been as influential on the lyrical content of songs as he has on the music itself, but the fact is that Elvis Songs number in the hundreds. Interestingly for our investigation, a large number of these songs feature Elvis Presley in a decidedly religious context. Elvis not only recorded religious music, he is the subject of religious music, though, as we shall see, of a markedly different sort.

— Graceland Gospel —

One of the characteristics of gospel music, particularly of the sort sung in southern churches like the ones I grew up in, is an emphasis upon the life, death, and resurrection of Jesus. These songs are gospel songs, at least in part, because they retell the stories found in the Christian Gospels, those first four books of the New Testament that follow Jesus from his birth to his resurrection and ascension. These gospel hymns are not just musical versions of the Jesus story, however, for what they add to the scriptural records is a personal testimonial about the meaning and significance of the life of Jesus for the individual. Gospel music often places the stories of Jesus in a decidedly personal context. It is not just that Jesus did and said the things recorded in scripture, but because of his deeds and words individual lives have been, and can be transformed. Gospel hymns, therefore, not only tell the story of Jesus, they offer testimonies from people who have been saved by Jesus.

It is not too much of a stretch to say that many of the songs written about Elvis Presley may be compared to gospel songs in that they share these two important characteristics. They tell the story of Elvis and of the impact of his deeds and words, and they tell how Elvis has touched the lives of individuals. They offer both stories and testimonies about Elvis. A good example of this type of Elvis gospel song is John Fogerty's 'Big Train (from Memphis)' (1985. *Centerfield*, Warner Brothers). This song attributes world-changing impact to Elvis and his music. The 'Memphis Train' (Elvis) changed the world when it came rolling through. Elvis was, the song seems to say, the harbinger of musical and cultural transformation. His life was of historical significance. Fogerty is telling the story of Elvis in much the way a gospel song would tell of Jesus. He is also, however, relating the importance of Elvis for his own personal life. For Fogerty, the significance of Elvis's life was that it meant that rock 'n' roll filled his own dreams, the sounds of Elvis were the sounds he heard as he closed his eyes at night. Elvis not only changed the world but he changed the life of an individual. This is Fogerty's testimony about what Elvis has done for him.

Subway to Sally's 'Elvis Lives' (1994. *Album 1994*, Costbar) also resembles a gospel testimonial. Indeed, the song is reminiscent of Easter hymns about the resurrected Jesus. These hymns often affirm the truth of Jesus' resurrection, of his victory over the grave, while at the same time proclaiming the importance of that event in the life of the present-day believer. It is because Jesus lives that the Christian can face trials and temptations, because Jesus overcame the grave that Christians can live with confidence and faith. Subway to Sally mirrors these aspects of Christian gospel music, but instead of Jesus this is a song of testimony and praise about Elvis. In the face of the coldest wind, or the darkest night, we are told, there is no reason to fear. Elvis is not dead. Elvis lives. He is with us even through our most difficult trials. Countless gospel hymns have said the same thing about Jesus. This is a true gospel testimony: because Elvis lives, I can face the valley of the shadow of death; fear and doubt are gone.

In Faith Hill's 'Bring Out the Elvis in Me' (1999. *Breathe*, Warner Brothers) the gospel of Elvis is once again presented in the form of a personal testimony. In this song Elvis is a symbol of sexual energy and musical freedom, a kind of energy and freedom that 1950s American culture had certainly not known before Elvis. In Hill's song, her fans, and her lover, bring out the spirit of Elvis that is, perhaps, suppressed inside her. They make her want to swing her hips, and dance and sing. She brings to the surface a part of herself that polite society insists we keep tightly under wraps. While it might be a stretch to say that there are many gospel hymns which appeal to the same spirit in regards to Jesus, that is sexual and musical freedom, the idea of Jesus inside us, moving and directing our lives is a common theme. Hill's song, in this sense, mirrors those gospel hymns that encourage us to let Jesus direct our lives, except we are being encouraged in this instance to put the spirit of Elvis in control.

For Patty Loveless in 'I Try to Think About Elvis' (1994. *When Fallen Angels Fly*, Sony), contemplation of Elvis constitutes an escape from a broken relationship. By thinking about Elvis, she seeks to free her mind from the object of its immediate and troubled desire. Like the injunction from Christian gospel music to 'turn you eyes upon Jesus,' Loveless turns her eyes to Elvis to free her spirit from its trials and temptations. Elvis offers a focus of meditation beyond the trials of the world. To think about Elvis is to reflect on something beyond the mundane, something that will turn our attention from our immediate surroundings, troubled and difficult, to something better. In this song Elvis represents a point of reflection beyond the troubles and trials of our life, an image, like Jesus, upon which we can look when we need guidance, salvation, or grace.

In Sister Hazel's 'Elvis' (2000. *Fortress*, Universal), the King of Rock 'n' Roll appears in the form of a religious icon. The song is about one of those tacky paintings of Elvis on black velvet, a medium also used to portray Christ, which serves as the point of salvation and hope as a relationship disintegrates. As possessions are split up between two former lovers, it is a velvet Elvis that constitutes the narrator's individuality. Elvis is what the narrator came into the relationship with, and what the narrator will take away. The narrator's former lover may have the dishes, the car, and the books, everything but the velvet Elvis. In this song, the kitsch painting of Elvis on velvet stands for, among other things, individuality and selfhood as well as the strength to transcend moments of crisis and loss.

The concept is the same in Vandal's 'Elvis Decanter' (1988. *Slippery When Ill*, Restless), in which an Elvis-shaped liquor bottle represents a relationship's end. As the bottle is emptied, so is the relationship. The more the liquor is consumed the less the lovers are together. The emptier the bottle, the emptier the affair. The decanter, an icon of Elvis, does not come to symbolize this loss, this ending, however, for the narrator manages to speak the name of Elvis in prayer. Somehow, though the listener cannot be sure how or why, the empty Elvis decanter offers the narrator hope and faith. The Elvis decanter offers the narrator a way to focus faith and hope.

Moist's 'Picture Elvis' (1994. *Silver*, Capital) also describes the importance of an Elvis icon, though one that occupies a place in the life of a person that is seemingly more personal and idiosyncratic than romance. Clipping a picture of Elvis from a book for unspoken reasons is a salvific experience for the character in this song. She clips the picture, trims it to fit in her wallet, and in doing so she has lived, she has experienced grace, she has tasted heaven.

Probably the most well-known example of what we have classified as Elvis gospel in popular music is found in Paul Simon's 'Graceland' (1986. *Graceland*, Warner Brothers). In this song, Elvis Presley's Memphis home constitutes a holy site, a destination for pilgrims. Simon's Graceland is a place of acceptance and, yes, grace. It is the focus of faith, the goal of our spiritual journey, like Mecca or Lourdes, or heaven itself. No one will be turned away. Poor boys and pilgrims from all over the world, traveling with their ghosts and demons, will find a welcome there.

Perhaps even more than Paul Simon's 'Graceland', however, I find that for me it is Dan Reeder's hauntingly hilarious 'Clean Elvis' (2004. *Dan Reeder*, Oh Boy Records) that expresses faith in the salvation offered by Elvis most clearly. Like haunted dreams of a fevered brain, or the delusions of a tormented schizophrenic, Reeder's enigmatic verses reveal the struggle and pain that come in the quest to know the true from the false and the real from the crazed. The narrator injects kryptonite into his brain, drives a car powered by nitroglycerine, believes in the unreal more than the real, and battles aliens from outer space. To this battle-weary veteran of intergalactic wars, Elvis is hope. 'Help me, Elvis!' is a cry for salvation and for love. Though 'Clean Elvis' appears to be on one level a humorous take on conspiracy theorists and Elvis fanatics, it makes its jokes with charm and understanding. The cry for help to Elvis strikes one as even more profound because it comes from the point of view of one who is in so much need. To such a one as this, surely only Elvis can save. It is a testimony of an individual's faith in Elvis. It is pure Graceland Gospel.

— Elvis Elegies —

Not all Elvis Songs are as confident in their proclamation that 'Elvis is Alive!' Indeed, Elvis's absence, that is his death, also appears as an important theme in many Elvis Songs. These songs are elegies to Elvis, songs expressing the sorrow felt over his death, the significance of his death for life in the world, and in some cases, harsh rejections of Elvis faith and of those who espouse it. Unlike the songs discussed in the previous sections, these songs offer up, not faith, but despair, anger, frustration, and loss. In Bryan Adams's 'Hey Elvis' (1996. *18 Till I Die*, A&M), for example, Elvis's absence is treated almost as an insult. It is as if everyone has been waiting for Elvis to arrive at a party, and he never shows up, as if Elvis, in dying, had stood us all up. In the mind of the narrator, Elvis has clearly been absent for too long. Everyone knows his story. We all know about his Cadillacs, about Lisa Marie, about TCB, and we all want to know when he is coming back. Every day that passes without his return is an insult to those who wait impatiently.

A similar theme is found in Dire Straits's 'Calling Elvis' (1991. *On Every Street*, Warner Brothers). Here, however, there seems to be a greater sense of despair, rather than disdain, at the fact of Elvis's absence. While the Bryan Adams song offers up an impatient complaint, this song sounds downright desperate. The narrator calls Elvis on the telephone as if he is expecting him to be home and does not get an answer. This leaves him all alone, a resident of the Heartbreak Hotel, without any hope of deliverance by Elvis. The loneliness one feels when a lover refuses to answer the telephone is transformed into a deeper, spiritual loneliness, when the absent lover is Elvis.

In 'Elvis is Dead' by MXPX (1998. *Let it Happen*, Tooth and Nail Records) the physical absence of Elvis, his death, stands in contrast with the claims of an inner voice that asserts that it is, in fact, the voice of Elvis. The experience of Elvis's death is made worse, not better, by the crazy assertion that he is alive. The loss of Elvis is itself a tragedy, but the insane claims that he is not dead make the tragedy worse, not better. The narrator knows the voice is lying, because he knows that Elvis is dead. Instead of hope and salvation those who would sing gospel songs about Elvis only bring more despair for they show themselves as either fools or liars. It is as if the narrator wants to say that the death of Elvis is bad enough, we only make it worse when we pretend that he is, in some way, still alive.

Likewise, in Kirsty MacColl's 'There's a Guy Works Down the Chip Shop (Swears He's Elvis)' (1991. single, Polydor), the death of Elvis shows the lie to the 'guy works down the chip shop swears he's Elvis.' The claim that Elvis is alive is for MacColl a straightforward lie, symbolic of the lie told by her lover. In both 'Elvis is Dead' and 'Chip Shop' the death of Elvis is juxtaposed with claims to the contrary.

In these songs faithlessness has taken hold. The fact of Elvis's death is made worse, not better, by those who falsely claim otherwise. Especially in MacColl's song, to claim that Elvis is alive is the epitome of an untruth.

Matthew Costello's 'Diggin' for Elvis' (2000. *Floating Festival Volume 2*, Planetary Records) is a song about an obsessed Elvis fan who must have Elvis, even if that acquisition comes at a terrible price. The absence of Elvis to one who admires him so, to one who suffers the Elvis blues, is not going to be resolved by a miraculous resurrection or return from heaven. He must take things into his own hands. He already owns all of Elvis's movies, drives a car like Elvis, has sideburns like Elvis, and takes pills like Elvis. But without Elvis he will always have the Elvis blues. The only solution is to go down to Graceland and dig up the King. Here, a rejection of the Elvis gospel takes the narrator's assessment of the perils of Elvis faith to their extreme. What a horrible thought, digging up Elvis out of love and devotion. Yet, the song says, this is what Elvis fanatics do when they claim that the King is still alive, when they crowd around his grave, as if expecting an Easter miracle.

This somber theme is magnified in 'Elvis Has Left the Building' by John Wesley Harding (1997. *It Happened Every Night*, WOW). In this song, Elvis's absence, his death, is symbolic of innocence lost. 'Elvis has left the building,' the famous words spoken to tell his audience that Elvis was not coming back for an encore, are now an expression of disappointment, regret, and loss. The innocence of the world is lost in the midst of nuclear threats and prejudice. Innocence is gone. Elvis has left the building. The potential annihilation of the human race as well as homophobic bigotry are marks of a world at its worst. Things are so bad that Elvis himself is no doubt glad to be gone from this world. There is no promise of an apocalyptic return, like Jesus on the clouds of glory. In this song, Elvis is gone, he is not coming back, and we are the worse for it. The refrain

'Elvis has left the building' is here reminiscent of the proclamation of Nietzsche's Zarathustra that 'God is dead.'
'Elvis has left the building' is a way of saying that things are
over, that opportunities have come to an end, that the book
has been closed. Elvis is gone and the world is finally
responsible for his absence.

In many songs about Elvis his absence and death are
seen as part of the larger tragedy that was his life. Warren
Zevon's song 'Porcelain Monkey' (2000. *Life'll Kill Ya*,
Artemis) describes Elvis's rise from poverty to fame as a
tragic rise. Already becoming a cultural joke at the time of
his death, already behind the times and rushing to catch
up with the revolution he had started, Elvis was surrounded by hangers-on who sought only their own benefit.
Elvis was a tragic figure even before he died, 'eating fried
chicken with his regicidal friends.'

In 'Elvis is Dead', the Forgotten Rebels (1988. *Surfin' on
Heroin*, Restless) manage to insult both Elvis and his faithful followers and fans in terms that offer no attempt at
understanding or appreciation. The fact of Elvis's death,
when asserted in this way, is itself an insult. 'Elvis is dead.
The big fat guy is dead . . . Millions of assholes mourned his
death. I'm gonna steal his body from the place of rest . . .
Elvis is dead . . . Spend your money on our records
instead.' This is the anti-gospel of Elvis. It is a rejection of
the claims of the gospel songs, a rejection of his significance, of his continued presence, and of his fans.

The explicit details about the truth of Elvis's current
condition are spelled out in The Inhalers' 'Rotting Elvis'
(2003. *Asses of Evil*, CD Baby). Despite reports of his death,
people claim that Elvis is still alive, that he was just spotted
at the 7-11. But the truth is he is rotting in the grave. He is
'rotting Elvis.' 'Sequined suit, all bloated and swollen . . .
growing mold on my pelvis.'

Living Colour's 'Elvis is Dead' (1990. *Time's Up*, Epic)
describes the sense of disgust directed to those who insist

that Elvis is alive, spotted at the shopping mall. Considering the fact of Elvis's death, the only way Elvis could be alive and at the mall would be as a kind of rotting zombie, Lazarus back from the grave but rotting and decayed, a rotting Elvis shopping for fresh fruit. Indeed, the tragic means of his passing are symbolic for Living Colour of the sad failure that was Elvis's life. The King died on his throne. Even Paul Simon's confession of faith in the shrine of Graceland is belittled in this song. Hinting at the unspoken racial homogeny that is Elvis fandom, made even more starkly apparent by the presence of mostly white Elvis fans in the midst of mostly black Memphis, Living Colour wonders if Simon's faith is misplaced. 'I've got a reason to believe we all won't be received at Graceland.' In these songs, disgust is directed, not just at the fools who would deem Elvis superior, but to Elvis himself. He is not only dead, he is rotting. He was not only a normal man, he was a joke.

The tragedy of Elvis's life and death is not completely at odds with his salvific activity, however. As Jesus transformed the world through the tragedy of his crucifixion, so Elvis may offer salvation through his sacramental death. It is the tragic aspects of Elvis's life and death that provide the gift of grace to the world. In 'Elvis Be True', Liz Phair (1996. *The Complete Girlysound Demos Disk 1*, Bliss and Fetish Records) is clearly in touch with both the tragic nature of Elvis's life and death and the ridiculous aspects of his continued posthumous presence on the cultural scene. It 'seems he can't die even if he wanted to.' The continued focus on Elvis is perplexing, however, for surely everyone knows that the King of Rock 'n' Roll was nothing but a 'junkie redneck.' Yet, this tragic and critical depiction of Elvis and the seemingly religious phenomena associated with Elvis, itself concludes with a prayer.

> Elvis be good to me
> Elvis be true

Elvis I love you
Elvis be near me.

U2 also describes the tragedy inherent in Elvis's spiritual presence in 'Elvis Ate America' (1995. *Original Soundtracks 1*, Island), in which a series of images and names are evoked to sum up the life, tragic death, and ambiguous influence of Elvis Presley. Elvis was white trash, out of his element in the world of private planes and Cadillac fleets. His wealth and fame corrupted him and killed him. 'Elvis ate America before America ate him.' This song ends, however, much like Liz Phair's 'Elvis Be True', in a way that suggests that this series of images associated with Elvis Presley, which describe the tragedy of his life, point beyond tragedy and toward hope and forgiveness. 'Forgive us, pray for us, (Elvis) Aaron Presley.'

John Gorka's 'That's Why' (1994. *Out of the Valley*, Highstreet) is a reflection on both the tragedy and the religious significance of Elvis, showing how the two aspects of the man are intimately connected. Elvis remains a part of life and culture, even after his death. He was a man transformed into a myth, a god-man like Jesus. 'The man part left and the rest stayed with.' Elvis's life and death were tragic, but it was a tragedy brought on by the needs and demands of the culture. Indeed, it is the same needs and demands that keep him alive. 'He's left the building, he's left the stage. He's left the building, but not the age. We asked too much we took his best. Couldn't live with him, can't let him rest.' We need Elvis. That need killed him and, ironically, resurrects him. Either way, dead or alive, Elvis is controlled by forces well beyond his control, by the forces that are constituted by the needs of others, by the needy others. The Stray Cats, in 'Elvis on Velvet' (1992. *Choo Choo Hot Fish*, Rhino), also articulate the way in which Elvis's tragedy is multiplied by the continuing infatuation with his person, and the continuing fanatical adoration of his fans.

His Graceland home, even his grave, is nothing more than a money-making enterprise. Claims that he is alive only serve to sell more records. As Elvis was consumed by his fans in life, so he is consumed in death.

— Ironic Invitationals —

When combined, the two competing themes found in Elvis Songs, his existence as a symbol of grace and salvation and the comic tragedy that many see in his life and ignoble death, can produce the most explicitly religious, yet most explicitly ironic, of Elvis Songs. It is as if the spiritual and tragic themes of Elvis's life and after-life may only be fully integrated in irony. The form that many such songs take is that of the Christian invitational. More pronounced in its level of testimony and its attempt to persuade the listener of the truth of that testimony, invitational hymns often occur at the conclusion of evangelistic services, when the emphasis is upon encouraging the listening audience to make a personal commitment to the Gospel that has been proclaimed. As it may be that the combination of the good news about Elvis and the shameful, ridiculous aspects of his life and death are best suited for an ironic treatment, so that irony is best expressed in this, the most explicit and direct of all gospel music forms.

A good example of this is seen in Mojo Nixon's 'Elvis is Everywhere' (1987. *Bo-Day-Shus!!!*, Enigma) in which the proclamations of the Elvis gospel are clearly expressed, but only in a decidedly ironic context. Mastering the rhythms and intonations of a gospel evangelist, the live recording of this song evokes a tent revival meeting where the gospel message is all about Elvis. 'Elvis is everywhere, Elvis is still the King. What I want you to see, is that big E's inside of you and me.' Elvis is inside everyone, we are told, regardless of race or age or gender. The seriousness of this proclamation of the spiritual presence of Elvis is shattered by the kind of ridiculous claims made about him, however. Elvis built the pyramids. Elvis built Stonehenge. People from outer space look just like Elvis, because Elvis is the apex of evolution. ('Why do you think they call it evolution? It's Elvis-lution!') Though it ends with a full-blown evangelistic altar call, an invitation to new life in Elvis that is an ironic poke at Elvis fans and at Christianity as well, there is nevertheless something convincing about these lines. The very force with which they are sung, and the cadences so reminiscent of summer revivals, makes them far more persuasive than perhaps they should be. The listener may be made to believe that Elvis is inside us. Or, that if he is not, he should be.

Likewise, Space's 'A Liddie Biddy Help From Elvis' (1995. *Tin Planet*, Uni) evokes the gospel call to 'have a little talk with Jesus.' Elvis is an angel from above, but a clearly ironic angel. More so than Mojo Nixon's song, this song evokes the tacky elements of Elvis's life as well as the conspiratorial elements espoused by the tabloids. This trashy, over-eating, conspiratorial Elvis still saves, however. Elvis, 'the burger eating King of Rock 'n' Roll,' is an angel sent from above. He is a joke, but a joke that saves. The ironic nature of Elvis's salvific works is also expressed in Frank Zappa's 'Elvis Has Just Left the Building' (1988. *Broadway the Hard Way*, Barking Pumpkin). Elements of the Elvis story are translated into heavenly language just as surely as Elvis must have been translated into heaven. 'The angels all love him, He brings them relief with droplets of moisture from his handkerchief.' Zappa's narrator, however, wants Elvis to return. Fat, tacky, past his prime – we will take him just the way he is.

Another example of an ironic proclamation of Elvis faith and an invitation to take up that faith is found in The Hancock Band's 'Elvis Saves' (2000. *The Hancock Band*, The

Orchard). Here, however, it is not so much Elvis who is mocked but rather the tabloid assertions that he is still alive. The narrator claims to have spotted Elvis pumping gas just yesterday. He was driving a white Cadillac, and bathed in heavenly light. There was a box of donuts in the back seat. Ironically, however, it is in this encounter with Elvis pumping gas, a tabloid-style sighting fit for the *National Enquirer*, that the narrator experiences salvation. 'Now the king he came and touched my hand. All at once I saw Graceland. And I went into a trance. I had to dance. In a sense I have been born again . . . Elvis saves.' Of course this song is ironic. Of course 'Elvis Saves' is not being said with a straight face. But it is being said, and the irony seems to give it life that it might not otherwise have. Many songwriters seem to want to talk about the religious experience, the saving grace, the sacramental presence, that is Elvis Presley. Irony provides an avenue for that expression more clearly than sincerity ever could.

— Conclusion —

A trend emerges. While I was unable to find much that looked like Elvis religion in the places I most expected to find it, in Graceland pilgrims and impersonator priests, among southern white- and euro-trash tourists, in Memphis, Tennessee, or Las Vegas, Nevada, it seems that the world of popular entertainment, of movies, novels, and music, provides a context for the growth of religious images associated with Elvis Presley. While it may not be the case that Elvis fans and impersonators constitute a new religious movement, while their interest in Elvis may be more mundane than spiritual, it seems that at least some segment of the popular culture wants there to be something religious going on around Elvis. Even if 'the cult of the King' is more wishful thinking than social fact, it seems that the idea of such a phenomenon has struck a nerve. Elvis may not be treated as a god by fans and impersonators, but his godhood has certainly been explored by filmmakers, novelists, and songwriters.

In all of these cases, in movies, in fiction, and in song, irony runs deep. Violent vision, ambiguous angel, Memphis Messiah, Jumpsuit Jesus – Elvis's depiction in all of these forms is a depiction rife with irony. Saint Elvis is a saint trapped by the violence and ignorance of his own American, and southern, culture. If Elvis saves it is through his flaws, not his strengths. A messiah from Memphis! Jesus in a Jumpsuit! By playing up the ridiculousness of religious claims about Elvis these images, ironically, serve to make Elvis appear to be that much more salvific. Like Jesus who heals by his stripes, so Elvis saves by his drug addiction, and his gluttony, and his tackiness.

Elvis Songs show this as well as anything, especially when they reach their zenith in what I have described as Ironic Invitationals, those songs intentionally structured after the form of evangelical invitationals and altar calls. As evangelical hymns arguably constitute one of the purest forms of Christian gospel music, their use by musicians and songwriters to proclaim the good news about Elvis is at once a humorous jab at both Christianity and at the idea of Elvis as a suitable replacement. However, the effect of this music, perhaps intentional, perhaps accidental, is to raise Elvis as much as it belittles Jesus. By the time Mojo Nixon is finished proclaiming that 'Elvis is Everywhere' I for one want to be a believer. I want to answer the altar call. It is the same thing that we see in books and movies. It is as if the saving grace of Elvis not only shines through the irony, but, indeed, shines because of the irony. To poke fun at the religious nature of Elvis is to establish Elvis's religious nature. While I expected to find Elvis worshipped as a saint by sincere and devoted fans and followers, a god for the

Elvis religion

tackiest side of American culture, instead it appears that Saint Elvis is more likely to be venerated – ironically, mind you – by those citizens of popular, post-modern culture for whom irony is already King. This ironic veneration is not exhausted in popular films, novels, and music, however, for it also lurks in other, less mainstream, eddies of popular culture. It is to these areas, the worlds of outsider art, the internet, and tabloid conspiracy theories that we now turn. In other words, by definition, things are about to get weirder.

6

Elvis in Art
Outsider Elvis and Graceland Too

— Graceland Too —

Holly Springs, Mississippi, is a sleepy little town located some forty miles southeast of Memphis, Tennessee. It is a town that was mercifully saved from total destruction during the Civil War and thus is the home of a fabulous number of grand antebellum homes and churches. These homes and churches are opened up for tourists during an annual festival of homes and, along with its picturesque courthouse square, serve to give Holly Springs an air of gentility. Indeed, Holly Springs looks so much like the stereotypical small southern town that it has served as the setting for more than one Hollywood production.

In addition to its grand antebellum homes, however, the city of Holly Springs has chosen to include another local attraction on the front page of its internet website. Though located in a small antebellum house just a few blocks from the historic town square, Graceland Too is hardly an expression of quiet southern charm. This is not to say that it is out of place, however, for southern towns have always had their share of eccentricities, and Graceland Too is nothing if not eccentric.

Elvis religion

On my first visit to Graceland Too I stopped off at the local Piggly Wiggly supermarket to ask directions. It was clear from the woman who was kind enough to assist me that Graceland Too was not exactly what many in the town would like to be the community's biggest draw. 'You want to go to Graceland Too?' she asked, incredulously. 'But there are so many other beautiful homes to see in Holly Springs.' Nevertheless, she gave me directions.

Graceland Too is a rather unimpressive, old house on a side street in Holly Springs. The cinder-block walls facing the front street are painted a bright shade of pink, and huge concrete lions, inexplicably painted blue and red, adorn either side of the front steps. On either side of the front door, artificial Christmas trees stand year round. One is white with blue decorations, the other blue, decked out in white. I suppose the trees are meant to be a tribute to Elvis's 'Blue Christmas'. A bell adorns the front door and is accompanied by hand-lettered signs to the effect that tours are available twenty-four hours a day, but that video cameras are strictly prohibited. It is the kind of place that makes you think twice before you ring the bell. The 'world's greatest Elvis museum' seems, at least at the front door, a bit overbilled.

This feeling does not subside when Paul MacLeod, proprietor of the establishment greets you at the door, at least it did not subside for me. Paul is a rather intense fellow in his sixties who, immediately after ushering you in, begins to bombard you with more information than any one person could possibly absorb. His saturation-bombing tour guide style is matched only by the interior of the house itself, in which every inch of space is crowded with material. For example, right inside the front door is a display, and by display I mean series of stacks, of old *TV Guide* magazines, not necessarily Elvis-themed. One of them has a picture of Lucy Lawless of *Xena, Warrior Princess* on the front, which seems to spark Paul's commentary to the effect that a woman who looked an awful lot like Xena once visited Graceland Too. As a matter of fact, I was assured, three women who looked exactly like the women from *Sex and the City* had just left moments before I arrived. Oh, and Cybil Shepherd's lawyers are members of Graceland Too.

Of course there is a lot of Elvis stuff on display, mostly of the lifesize cardboard cutout, poster, or publicity photo sort. There are baseball caps with Elvis's name on them and there is one wall on which a picture of Elvis is draped by curtains to resemble an icon in a church alcove. A gold suit, like the one made famous by Elvis hangs in one corner, right above a pair of old sneakers, apparently spray painted blue. Old Elvis LP covers are displayed here and there. I suspect that if they had any collectable value it is rapidly deteriorating due to the manner of their display. Paul seems more interested in other things, however, like the remnants of a cast iron mailbox post that he claims was 'karate chopped' in the middle of the night by what he describes as 'Japanese Chinese girls from Memphis State University.' He says, incredulously, that he only laughed at the police when they asked if he wanted to press charges. Who would dare press charges against someone that could 'karate chop' an iron post?

Apparently, much of what MacLeod has he is keeping to himself, like, for example, a film of Elvis, supposedly taken by Paul and his son, Elvis Aaron Presley MacLeod, on the day that Elvis died. When I asked him about the footage he first looked quickly out the front window to verify that no one was listening and then told me that the footage he had would make me drop dead if he showed it to me. Much to my relief, he never offered to let me see it, though he promised that if I ever came back he might bestow the honor upon me. What he did show me, however, were photo albums filled with snapshots of Graceland Too visitors. There was a photo of a twelve-day-old Elvis impersonator as well a photo of a 102-year-old, female impersonator. There was also a picture of Tom Cruise's dog. (Apparently Cruise must have taken the picture, because his likeness does not appear.) Other pictures were of yard rakes raking what seemed to be play money. Paul indicated that those pictures were symbolic of the fact that he was 'raking in the money.'

The 'TV room' as MacLeod calls it, has, in addition to more posters, LP covers and cutouts, three television sets that, it is claimed, record television programs twenty-four hours a day. These tapes are then stored in bins that fill up much of the room. Since Paul claims to be attempting to record every reference to Elvis broadcast on the airwaves, I was careful not to mention the existence of five hundred channel cable or satellite dish connections and digital recorders. He seemed blissfully unaware of the existence of anything more than the old 'Big Three' networks and I was content to let him remain so. He did, however, stop recording on one set long enough to show a recording he had made of his own interview on a Memphis news program. For one surreal moment I stood in the TV room of Graceland Too and watched a video of MacLeod giving the same tour, practically verbatim, that he had just been giving to me.

Another room of the house is filled with huge sheets of plywood upon which have been affixed photographs of visitors to the museum: photographs that must number in the thousands are on display, though I thought I perceived that many of the photographs were duplicates, so I cannot say for certain that the number of photographs accurately represents the number of visitors to the museum, though Paul claims that he has pictures developed four times a day.

The entire tour can sometimes take up to two hours. On one occasion I made the mistake of dropping by with only about half of that time available for the tour. I was informed, in no uncertain terms, that when I came back I should be prepared to stay for the duration. After the full two-hour tour, indeed after a shortened forty-five-minute tour, I am exhausted. It is hard to be sure what exactly it is that I have just seen and heard. Part of this uncertainty is brought on by the simple fact that Paul MacLeod, in both his spoken presentation and his exhibits, throws a lot of things at you, sometimes in a less than coherent fashion. There is also the question, of course, of how much of what one is told is legitimate and how much is, though no doubt believed by Paul, less than accurate. (Bill Clinton dropping by with a box of diamond rings and a bag of guns seems just beyond what I am willing to accept.) The biggest problem, however, is that I am just not sure what to make of Graceland Too as a whole. While it has been treated in some accounts as a sort of religious shrine dedicated to Elvis or as a holy site along the pilgrimage from Memphis to Tupelo, there seems to me to be little about Graceland Too itself that exhibits these characteristics. Is it possible that some tourists come to Graceland Too as part of a religious pilgrimage? Of course it is possible. This does not mean that there is anything religious about Paul MacLeod's motives or about the place itself.

MacLeod, I think, is more likely to describe Graceland Too as a museum meant to keep Elvis's legacy alive, and it certainly has some of the qualities that one would associate with a museum, especially the kind of private museums and curiosity cabinets that were all the rage in the nineteenth century and that still can be found in people's homes and in store fronts. Indeed, when Paul gave a presentation at the University of Mississippi in 1995 these were just the kinds of themes that he struck. As recorded in the short film *In Search of Elvis: Music, Race, Art, Religion*, edited by Vernon Chadwick, Paul reported on that occasion that his entire house – every room from floor to ceiling – was dedicated to Elvis, 'the greatest entertainer and humanitarian ever born.' He described his collection as consisting of everything from a program from the Humes High School

talent contest of April 9, 1953, which Elvis won, to thumb
tacks with Elvis's picture on them.

The theme of many of the exhibits, and the theme of
MacLeod's tour, however, makes the interpretation of
Graceland Too as a museum a little strained, however, for
much of the tour is devoted, not to the supposed subject of
the museum, namely Elvis Presley, but to Graceland Too
itself. The exhibits, after all, include photographs of the
museum's visitors and a video presentation about, not
Elvis, but Graceland Too. One of MacLeod's favorite items
to point out to guests is a homemade sign that hangs in his
entranceway and reads:

THE UNIVERSE'S
GALAXY'S
PLANET'S
WORLD'S
ULTIMATE
NUMBER ONE
ELVIS FANS
PAUL AND ELVIS
AARON PRESLEY
MACLEOD
AT GRACELAND TOO
1853
T.C.B.

Indeed, as much as Paul MacLeod describes the character of Elvis in glowing terms, he is also quite insistent
about his own level of dedication. A repeated claim is that
in order to maintain a record of the life, times, and legacy
of Elvis Presley, Paul himself was called upon to make great
sacrifices. His own sacrifices are then described in at least
as much detail as Elvis's accomplishments. For example,
consider this from his University of Mississippi address:

> You ask me what I gave up? I was lucky enough to give
> up my time to go ahead and devote myself to Elvis. And

I gave up another house that I owned that was paid for, a ranch-style home. I had $120,000 in customized furniture in it. I had $30,000 in furniture that we're livin' in now from Graceland Too. I had a Harley-Davidson motorcycle, a boat, a camper, a swimming pool, all paid for, $30,000 worth of diamond rings and watches I got rid of, a gold Cadillac, a Cadillac limousine with VIPs and wraparound bars and the whole works. To top that off, my wife was with me for twenty-two years, seven days a week, twenty-four hours a day, and she finally told me to make a decision – either her or the Elvis collection. And I told her 'bye, and that's the last time I seen her. (Chadwick 1997: 162)

Of course I recognize that part of Paul's emphasis upon his own sacrifices, as well as his own fame, is an effort to illustrate to his patrons how great is his dedication to Elvis. At some point, however, he seems to have crossed a line. Graceland Too seems less and less about Elvis, and more and more about Paul MacLeod and Graceland Too. It is, as a friend wrote on her comment card after visiting the place, a truly post-modern museum, a museum dedicated first and foremost to itself.

After many visits to this museum shrine, however, I have come to think of Graceland Too as neither shrine nor museum, but rather a work of art. MacLeod himself has hinted at this, for example in his description of some of the original pieces of his own work that are included in his collection. Of particular interest is a lamp made from a globe of the earth and MacLeod's interpretation of its significance as offered at the University of Mississippi.

When Elvis died, believe it or not, I came up with the idea of a lamp for him after I attended his funeral and everything. I'm gonna put in a switch to a motor that will make the globe of the world go around because in Elvis's fans' eyes, it's become ELVIS'S WORLD now . . . I'm going to drill holes around this globe and put a miniature music box inside of it that would play *Welcome to My World, Can't Help Falling in Love*, and *I Did It My Way* 'cause this man did it his way.

I covered the state of Mississippi here where he was born with a heart shaped 'I Love Elvis' pin. He was born in Mississippi, but he died in Tennessee.

I got the red teardrops in it because eighteen years ago this world cried when this man died.

I got the 'Number One' on it representin' Elvis fans worldwide – of all, being number one in that man's eyes.

I got the red light bulb in it because it represents how the media around the world caught fire when they learned of Elvis's passin'.

I done the lampshade in five coats of black because it represents the blackest day in Elvis fans' history.

I got the '8/16/77' representin' for the day he died.

I got the crown on top because his recordings are up to a billion and a half and he was THE KING OF ROCK 'N' ROLL, THE KING OF ENTERTAINMENT.

And I done a cross with me and my son's pictures on them and everything. A lot of people been askin' why we done that. What it is, he was THE KING OF ROCK 'N' ROLL, THE KING OF ENTERTAINMENT, but I betcha two dollars he's with THE KING OF KINGS and you won't find another Elvis fan that will disagree with me on that. Yeah. (Chadwick 1997: 165–166)

In a sense, the entirety of Graceland Too may be seen as another version of his Elvis lamp. It is an interactive, living, breathing, house-sized, Elvis-themed, piece of art, more akin to the elaborate creations that some of our eccentric neighbors have built in their front yards than to Lourdes or the Smithsonian. The elements of the house, from the attempt to mimic Graceland's wall and lion sculptures, to the Elvis collectables that fill up every inch, are like the elements of the lamp. They are all 'representin'' something important about Elvis Presley. To understand Graceland Too we need to understand it in this way, not as a shrine or a museum but as a work of art. To discover the religious significance of Graceland Too, if there is any, we have to pursue the issue, not by assuming that Paul MacLeod has either created a religious shrine to Elvis or that Graceland Too offers some sort of factual account of Elvis's life and significance. Both of these have been assumptions of journalists and scholars and both have missed the mark.

— Andy Warhol and Velvet Elvis —

Of course, Elvis as art is as old as the arrival of Elvis on the popular scene half a century ago. There was always something about his looks, those pouting lips, that hair, those eyes, that made it certain that Elvis's look, as well as his sound, would be artistically immortalized. The most famous example of Elvis in the visual arts is undoubtedly found in Andy Warhol's series of Elvis screen-prints taken from that less-than-artistic movie *Flaming Star*. In these prints Elvis is presented, rather atypically, in the costume and pose of a Hollywood cowboy. Accentuated by color and duplication in Warhol's prints, Elvis's look is at once wide-eyed innocent and menacing. His legs spread apart and his gun pointing straight ahead appear more erotic than adventurous. If the costume and pose are atypical for the King of Rock 'n' Roll, the impression made by the image, that of a boyishly innocent yet sexually threatening young man, is certainly not. It captures what was loved, and hated, about Elvis Presley in the 1950s and 1960s.

The other image most closely associated with Elvis and the visual arts is that of the velvet Elvis. These prints of Elvis, usually close-ups, printed on black velvet, have come to stand for the epitome of bad taste in art. Produced mostly by nameless artisans and either given away as prizes at carnivals or sold by roadside art dealers from the back of pickup trucks, these paintings of Elvis barely qualify for most people as art at all. These prints picture Elvis at all stages of his career, including occasionally an image from one of his movies, but the most common are those depicting Elvis late in his life. Often, a single tear is shown flowing down his cheek as he sings into a microphone and gazes into the distance. These paintings are, almost universally, poorly done. However, perhaps because they share certain stylistic elements with paintings of Jesus and the Virgin Mary, they can be evocative of a certain reverential, if tacky, attitude toward their subject. For most people, Warhol and velvet probably sum up Elvis and the visual arts. This perception could not be more wrong, however. We just have to look beyond the world of the mass produced, whether that be Warhol's tweaking of an image from a Hollywood film to make it suitable for framing or silkscreening on a t-shirt, or paintings of Elvis on velvet, made quickly and intended to be sold cheap and fast to the uncultured masses. We have to look, not only outside the world of fine art, and outside the world of consumer-driven art, and outside the world of folk art. We have to look just plain old outside.

— Outsider Elvis —

'Outsider Art' is a category of art that is usually reserved for art that exhibits certain qualities. This art differs from 'fine art' because it is not the product of a university or art-school setting nor is it intended to be displayed in museums, though it sometimes happens that this is the case. It is not 'commercial art' because the primary motive of the artist is not to make something to sell, though often that is what happens. It is not technically 'folk art' because it is not the result of traditional training. Outsider art tends to be idiosyncratic and self-taught, and, in the southern

United States, it is often constructed and displayed out-side, more often than not in someone's front yard, or in many cases, on the body of their car. In my own life, such outsider artists I have known include a local preacher who converted his back yard into the Garden of Eden, complete with the tree of knowledge of good and evil. This tree was a metal bucket filled with concrete from which protruded metal poles each ending in such dangerously deadly fruit as a light bulb, a telephone receiver, and a television remote control. Likewise is the fellow who lives just a few miles from me in central Alabama who built round buildings out of limestone found on his farm, including a prayer chapel and a home for his daughter and her husband, as well the fellow who lives just down the road and has constructed a huge metallic gargoyle to guard the entrance to his home. Once you open your eyes, it is clear that these artists are, like Elvis, everywhere.

Howard Finster

Howard Finster of Summerville, Georgia, was a Baptist preacher who, at an early age, felt a call from God to pro-duce sacred art. The result was his elaborate *Paradise Garden*, in which he converted his home and surrounding environs into a tableau for his creations. This jumbled mix of old buildings, overgrown vegetation, junk cars, and Fin-ster's art was, in its heyday in the late 1980s, a truly remarkable example of an individual's conversion of his entire surroundings into an expression of his artistic vision. Driven by his strong evangelical faith and by a strong sense of national pride, Finster's work is by its very nature didactic. He meant to educate and transform rather than just entertain.

Alongside biblical characters and figures from American history, Finster included Elvis as a recurring icon in his work. Indeed, Finster claimed to have had visions of Elvis and perceived the musician as a sacred figure worthy of sacred art. As a matter of fact, Elvis often occurs in Finster's art in a decidedly religious context. For example, on the back side of a wood cutout of Elvis dated February 13, 1999, Finster wrote 'Jesus is coming in great power. Be ready around the clock.' In his *Youth of Elvis* a young Elvis is depicted against a background of heavenly figures, angels, and stars. Equally interesting are his images of Elvis as a young boy, fitted with angel wings. In all of these works, a youthful Elvis stands wide eyed and ready to face the world. And in all of these works Finster places this Elvis in the context of a heavenly plan. An exception to his usual youthful painting of Elvis, his *Happy 200th Anniversary Tennessee* includes a photograph of Elvis in a white jumpsuit. The photograph is placed as the central facet of this tribute to Tennessee, reaching its peak in angelic and astral visions that seem to accentuate Elvis as the meeting point between heaven and earth.

Finster's religious associations with Elvis were most clearly expressed in 1995 in the context of a sermon delivered at the International Conference on Elvis Presley sponsored by the University of Mississippi and recorded in Vernon Chadwick's *In Search of Elvis*. In his own inimitable language, rich with southernisms, Finster delivered a 'Sermon on Alvis' in which he explained the role of 'Alvis' in his own life and in the larger plan of God. For Finster, it seemed that Elvis had always been a part of his life. As Finster served local churches in one place after another, he heard stories of Elvis being here and there. Elvis, it seemed to him, was everywhere. In his own words, 'He's been in my life ever since he's been in the world just about it . . . There's been one thing in my whole lifetime that I heard about and looked at and listened to was Alvis Presley. And he finally was part of me, part of my ministry' (Chadwick 1997: 204).

Elvis was, Finster claimed, a folk artist like himself. Elvis did things his own way, without training and education, and was thus able to truly carry out the work of God. Though Finster never saw Elvis when he was alive, he does claim to have been visited by Elvis in his garden, after Elvis had died. This spiritual vision of Elvis Presley was not shocking to Finster because it had long been clear to him that God had sent Elvis to the world for a special purpose. Indeed, Finster compares Elvis most directly to Abraham Lincoln, Thomas Edison, and the Wright Brothers, modern-day figures used by God to transform the world. God, according to Finster, 'took a likin' to him' (Chadwick 1997: 208) and prepared Elvis for a special life. The role Elvis played in Finster's life and in God's plan is represented in Finster's art by his works devoted to Elvis, which in turn have served to confirm Elvis's holy calling for Finster. After completing *The Youth of Alvis by Howard Finster*, Finster claims that he turned the piece over to examine the back.

I just turned around and I seen an image of what I though was an image of Jesus on the back of that. And I couldn't hardly believe it. And I think to myself, 'Am I seein' things?' And every one of these I start right here and do that just like you see it on the back. And I put on there 'The front face line makes the back face line and you have two faces with one line.' . . . And that's not somethin' that I figured out. And it's not somethin' that a folk artist done. I had nothin' to do with it. I just seen it. And it meant somethin' to me. It's tryin' to tell me somethin' about Alvis. There he was on one side and that's how close Jesus was with him on the other side. And that Jesus loves all people. (Chadwick 1997: 213–214)

Joni Mabe

By her own account, Joni Mabe did not become an Elvis fan until she was twenty years old. In August of 1977, while washing her automobile, Mabe's life was changed, however. On the day of Elvis's death, elbow deep in soapy water and listening to an Elvis tribute on the radio, Mabe would be transformed into the 'Elvis Babe.' After 1977, Mabe says that she became obsessed with Elvis. Every holiday became Elvis-themed. There were Elvis jack-o-lanterns on Halloween and Elvis Christmas trees at Christmas. She earned a Master of Fine Arts degree from the University of Georgia with a thesis devoted to, of course, Elvis. After her first trip to Graceland, too poor to afford any souvenirs, Mabe began making her own Elvis objects. These, combined with a toenail she claims to have found on the floor of Graceland's jungle room that she thinks, maybe, belonged to Elvis, soon evolved into The Elvis Room, a traveling display of memorabilia, original art, and relics from the life of Elvis Presley. The Elvis Room would later be transformed into Joni Mabe's Traveling Panoramic Encyclopedia of Everything Elvis. Once the collection became too big to move, Mabe found a permanent location for it in an old family home, renamed The Loudermilk Boarding House Museum, located in North Georgia.

On display at the Boarding House, which Mabe is in the process of converting into a bed and breakfast (The World's First Bed and Elvis) are some thirty thousand items, including the now-famous toenail, as well as an Elvis wart that was given to her by the Memphis doctor who removed it from Elvis's wrist in 1957 or 1958. By her own description, given at the University of Mississippi and recorded in Chadwick's *In Search of Elvis*, her collection contains:

> Elvis whiskey decanters, Elvis collectors' plates, Elvis costumes, Elvis lamps, Elvis clocks and watches, an Elvis bedspread, Elvis pillows, Elvis T-shirts, Elvis mugs, Elvis caps, an Elvis 1964 jukebox with fifty Elvis

45 records, Elvis bedroom slippers, Elvis towels, Elvis knives, Elvis cologne, Elvis shoestrings, Elvis sweat, Elvis albums, tabloids with stories of 'Elvis on Mars', 'Nixon Grooming Elvis for President', 'Elvis Sightings', 'Elvis is Alive', 'Elvis is Dead at 58', 'Elvis Tribe in Africa', 'Smelvis – Cow Paddy in Shape of Elvis's Face', 'Elvis in Coffin', 'Elvis Hiding in Swiss Alps with Kennedy and Hitler', – and all things and anything related to Elvis. (Chadwick 1997: 154)

Mabe's original art includes such pieces as *Elvis Mosaics*, which were inspired by her visit to Italy. Lithographs on paper, adorned with acrylic, glitter, rhinestones, sequins, lace and, of course, black velvet, these works at once seem to be reminiscent of fine religious art and the most tasteless bits of roadside tourist junk. One suspects this is just the mixture that Mabe is going for. Another important piece by Mabe is her *Elvis Prayer Rug* that, she claims, is meant to be taken into the bathroom as part of a forty-day prayer ritual. When accompanied by a $40 donation to Mabe, said ritual will cure arthritis or high blood pressure.

There is, however, no single piece of her own artwork, no single Elvis relic, and no single piece of mass-produced Elvis collectabilia that stands at the core of Mabe's art. Her work is really the collection itself, a madcap cabinet of curiosities devoted to all things Elvis. The original pieces, the relics, the tacky knick-knacks, must be taken together. It is the collection as a whole, rather than any one of its parts, which really comprises her art. She is a collector, like her hero P. T. Barnum, and even the greatest pieces serve the whole. 'The wart is like my Jumbo and the toenail is like the Fiji Mermaid' (Chadwick 1997: 156).

The Twenty-Four Hour Church of Elvis

First of all, it should be noted that Portland, Oregon's Twenty-Four Hour Church of Elvis was not open twenty-four hours. Nor was it really a church. It was, instead, a kind of kitschy cabinet of curiosities, filled with bits of Barbie dolls and assorted memorabilia from the 1970s and 1980s. Before it was called the Twenty-Four Hour Church of Elvis the establishment was called Where's the Art? – The World's First Coin Operated Art Gallery, which was perhaps a more fitting name, if not a more profitable one. For $5 a couple could participate in a wedding at the church that was not a legally binding ceremony. Legal weddings cost $25. The happy couple could also have been serenaded by Elvis for an extra $25, but in this case 'Elvis' was the pseudonym for a Portland street performer who was known for singing Elvis tunes at the top of his lungs while wearing a blue cape and, I should add, looking nothing like Elvis. In addition, a quarter would initiate the operation of The Mystery of the Spinning Elvi, a contraption that consisted of various likenesses of Elvis that would spin to contact the spirit of the King. The King's presence, then, would either bless wedding vows or offer up fortunes.

The 'pastor' of the establishment was Stephanie Pierce, who likes to call herself an 'Artist to the Stars.' Reports are that Stephanie displayed a rather intense attitude toward tours of her establishment, getting angry when new patrons dared to interrupt tours in progress. Apparently the church has recently fallen on hard times and been forced to close, leaving Stephanie to sell off her collection at a local flea market.

— More Elvis Art —

Of course, not all visual art devoted to Elvis Presley falls into the category of the outsider exhibition, cabinet of curiosities, Graceland Too, Howard Finster, Joni Mabe, Twenty-Four Hour Church of Elvis model. A surprising number of artists have turned their attention to producing works of Elvis art with more mainstream, if not necessarily more critical, appeal. There are countless fan artists who lovingly paint portraits of their idol, often in familiar stage poses or in scenes from movies. These often get showcased on Elvis fan club websites and regularly appear for sale on eBay.

There are also, however, many artists who, for diverse reasons beyond those attributable to fan infatuation, produce works in which Elvis has a central role. Many of these very intentionally evoke religious style and imagery. A good example of this are pieces that were recently on display at Birmingham, Alabama's Naked Art Gallery's What Would Elvis Do? exhibit. There, one could see Eileen Kiernan's wonderful mosaic table entitled *The Last Supper (Elvis)*. This table top, placed upon an antique sewing machine frame, features a tile mosaic image of Elvis flanked by Priscilla and Colonel Tom Parker. Elvis seems to be enjoying a turkey leg, which he apparently plans to wash down with a bottle of Jack Daniels whiskey and follow with pills from the multiple pill bottles scattered on the table. In addition, the Naked Art Gallery featured Katy Dement's *Angel Elvis*, a lighted wall-sconce made from recycled paper and covered in bees' wax which shows a young, swimsuited Elvis Presley, arms lifted, and adorned with angel wings. There is also Ceci Smith's *Gladys and Child* which depicts a baby Elvis (though side-burned and in a white jumpsuit) in the arms of his mother Gladys.

— Conclusion —

What can we now say, after considering the work of Paul MacLeod, Howard Finster, Joni Mabe, Stephanie Pierce, Eileen Kiernan, Katy Dement, and Ceci Smith, about the

Elvis religion

place of Elvis Presley in the world of the visual arts, especially in regards to his relationship to religious belief? I think that several observations are called for at this point.

First, it is important to note the idiosyncratic nature of the majority of works that we have examined here. By definition, outsider art will always be idiosyncratic and subject to the life story, cultural setting, economic situation, and philosophical worldview of the artist, so it may seem at first that this observation hardly warrants our attention. However, I think that it is important that we keep this in mind as we consider the religious nature of Elvis art. What I mean by this is that it is probably best if we try to avoid any big, generalized, conclusions about the place of Elvis in art. It is clear that Elvis has a place in the work of, for example, Howard Finster. It is even more obvious that Elvis Presley has a place in the work of Joni Mabe, and especially Paul MacLeod. As a matter of fact, we should probably say that Elvis is the driving inspiration behind their productions. It would be a mistake, however, to look for a common theme in the work of these three artists, or a common role that is played by the figure of Elvis Presley.

This emphasis upon the idiosyncratic nature of the work leads me to my second observation, namely that in the artists that we have examined there are differing mixtures of sincerity and irony at play when it comes to the importance of Elvis Presley. Howard Finster, for example, seems to have produced his Elvis-themed artwork with the utmost sincerity. For Finster, Elvis was clearly understood as a religious figure whose life's work was a part of God's ultimate plan. Finster associated Elvis with religious themes because Finster saw Elvis from a religious point of view. Elvis was an angel, a messenger of God. Elvis even appeared to Finster in the midst of his garden, a garden that was, in many respects and at least in part, a shrine to the life and memory of Elvis.

Something very similar, I believe, can be said about Paul MacLeod, though it is clear that MacLeod is far less religious than was Finster. While MacLeod has made note of his belief that Elvis was a righteous man of God who is undoubtedly now in heaven with the King of Kings, his admiration for Elvis tends to be more secular in its orientation. MacLeod sees Elvis in terms of his great talent, his worldwide fame, his kindness and generosity, and his love and devotion to his fans. Elvis is not so much a saint in the eyes of MacLeod as he is the world's greatest entertainer who also happened to be a very decent man. Despite this difference in the religious significance of Elvis, however, MacLeod, like Finster, is deadly serious in his estimation of Elvis. His work of art, Graceland Too, flows from a genuine devotion to the King.

It seems that the work of Stephanie Pierce, the Twenty-Four Hour Church of Elvis, is something entirely different however. Though it closely resembles Graceland Too in the way that it features kitschy souvenirs and an emphasis upon the collection of even the most mundane items, it nevertheless seems to have a very different approach to Elvis Presley. Pierce has even stated that if she had known her exhibit would attract so many Elvis fans she would have called it something else. It is seems clear that the characterization of her establishment as a church is meant as an ironic joke. The place of Elvis is equally played for laughs.

Joni Mabe, on the other hand, seems to fall somewhere between these two extremes of devotion and irony. Her devotion to Elvis is clearly sincere, and I think she would challenge anyone who said otherwise. However, she is certainly aware that by taking that devotion to the extreme she has crossed over into the territory of the ironic. This seems especially true when one considers her treatment of Elvis's toenail and wart as holy relics or when one remembers that her prayer rug is meant to be used in the bathroom. Mabe may have just as much devotion to Elvis as Finster and MacLeod, but her devotion is expressed in a self-consciously ironic way that would be foreign to either of them. (Though, MacLeod's Graceland Too strikes most visitors as being equally ironic, it is, I think, safe to say that most of that irony is lost on MacLeod. That is, unless he is better at making a joke than I give him credit for.) Likewise, Mabe offers up just as much irony in her reverence of Elvis as does Pierce, though it seems clear that unlike Pierce, Mabe's irony is an expression of her genuine devotion.

All of this leads to a third observation, this time in regard, not to the artists themselves, but to their visitors and patrons. Specifically, I want to say that we have to recognize the same kinds of idiosyncratic motivations in the patrons of Elvis art as we recognize in the artists. Furthermore, we have to recognize that both devotion and irony play critical roles in this motivation. Some people buy and display Elvis art in their homes and offices because they are Elvis fans and like to have images of Elvis on display for their own enjoyment or as a way to participate in the social life of an Elvis fan community. Some people display Elvis art because they think it is funny. Their inclusion of Elvis icons is meant as an ironic joke. And, yes, some display Elvis art as a form of religious devotion to Elvis. It is important for us, however, not to assume that one of these explanations is more likely than another.

I make this point, at least in part, to again call into question the claims that Graceland Too, and, for that matter, the Twenty-Four Church of Elvis, constitute evidence for the birth of an Elvis cult or a new Elvis religion. This is simply not the case. Some people may have visited these attractions with religious motivations, especially perhaps the one that billed itself as a church, but if so they probably left disappointed, especially those who went looking for a church. The joke, in that case, was on them. Many people visit these sites because they are Elvis fans and wish to learn more about the King, or share in the experiences of other Elvis fans. Others, however, and I suspect that many return visitors fall into this category, visit these sites as a joke. Whether Paul MacLeod realizes it or not, many of his visitors are students from the University of Mississippi who like to get a little tipsy, drive up to Holly Springs, and have a good laugh at the expense of Elvis. Are there certain religious connotations associated with a pilgrimage to Graceland Too? Yes, I suppose there are. However, it is precisely those religious connotations that serve to constitute the heart of the joke.

7

Elvis on the Internet

Presleyterians,
Eighth Day Transfigurists, and
the Dizgraceland Chapel

It was not while riding the tour bus up the front drive of Graceland mansion, nor while watching an Elvis tribute artist perform on stage in Las Vegas, that this whole Elvis thing most made sense to me. It was not in the fictional accounts of Elvis flickering across my TV screen or being fleshed out in the words of a novel that I was brought closest to the King. Likewise, it was not any song about Elvis or any work of art in tribute to Elvis in which the truth about Big E first started to come into focus. No, it happened late at night, with family long asleep, the lights out, while surfing the web. There is a realization that strikes one sometimes while surfing the net late at night as you come to understand that someone out there has written a detailed synopsis of every episode of *The Simpsons*, that someone has cataloged Bob Dylan's every concert performance for the last forty years, that someone collects those troll figures with the neon colored stand-up hair, that someone, maybe a lot of someones, believe that the earth is hollow and inhabited by miniature mastodons, and that someone actually does have a collection of lunchbox- and thermos-shaped salt-and-pepper shakers. (I only have the one, honest.) It really is a strange world out there, there really are a lot of different people, with a lot of different points of view and a lot of different beliefs and concerns and cares and worries. Some of those people have a lot to say about Elvis Presley.

The internet makes it clear that there is no overwhelming consensus among computer literate, apparently moderately educated, English speaking, western individuals when it comes to such questions as the origins of the world and the nature of reality. Nor is there much of a consensus about ethics, aesthetics, politics, or economics, not to mention extraterrestrials, giant lake monsters, and eight-foot-tall hairy hominids. Religion, the nature and existence of god, the means of salvation – there is no reason to even look for agreement here. There is, instead, diversity. So while Elvis devotion, or more correctly, religious symbolism associated with Elvis Presley, may seem odd or strange when juxtaposed with a big, abstract, and seemingly monolithic entity like CHRISTIANITY, it doesn't appear quite so strange when placed in the context of the real world in which Christians can't agree on whether to accept or reject Darwin's theory of evolution or come to any agreement about the role of UFOs in God's plan for salvation. What the internet makes clear is that interest in Elvis, both religious and non-religious, is not really an aberration, but instead part of the incredible variety of phenomena, religious and secular, that make up everyday life in this weird world of democratic and technological individualism that many of us call home.

Fortunately, when it comes to Elvis, one doesn't even have to stay up late or look too aggressively to find his presence on the internet, however. Any person who uses email regularly enough, or who spends enough time surfing the internet, is sooner or later bound to come into contact with the comparison between Elvis and Jesus, a ubiquitous list of similarities between the King of Kings and the King of

Rock 'n' Roll. Having made the rounds of the email chain-letter circuit, this list also appears on countless websites. Though I have not been able to determine its exact point of origin, one of the most commonly cited sources is www.infidels.org. According to this list, there are enough parallels between Jesus and Elvis to rule out mere coincidence as the explanation. Jesus said 'Love thy neighbor.' Elvis, conveying the same message but in his own unique style, said 'Don't be cruel.' Jesus was accompanied by a dozen apostles. Elvis was followed by his entourage, the Memphis Mafia, which also had twelve members. Jesus was resurrected. Elvis had a 'Comeback Special' on television, and has been seen many times following his death. Jesus is described as being transformed so that his appearance was like lightning and his clothes were as white as snow. Elvis, of course, wore white jumpsuits and used the lightning bolt as his symbol. Jesus was born in humble surroundings. Elvis was born in Mississippi. One can't be sure who should be most insulted by these comparisons, Elvis fans, Christians, or Mississippians. What is clear, however, is that these comparisons are meant as a joke, and probably as a joke at the expense of all the parties involved.

Elvis's presence in the world of the internet is not only in the form of a joke, however. Indeed, there are some internet sites devoted in a very serious way to the subject of Elvis Presley. One of these, www.elvis-presley.com is owned by Elvis Presley Enterprises, Incorporated and is the official site of Elvis Presley and Graceland. It provides information about upcoming events and matters of interest to those who may be planning to visit Elvis's Memphis home or who just want to stay informed of the latest Elvis-related news. In addition there are numerous unofficial websites devoted to Elvis Presley, including official Elvis fan club sites, many of which are approved by Elvis Presley Enterprises.

Elvis religion

A further look, however, shows that the image of Elvis Presley is not even close to being exhausted by these officially sanctioned sites. Indeed, a quick survey of the internet reveals that Jesus and Elvis have at least one other thing in common. They are both the subject of veneration by churches, and those churches are, in both instances, split into various sectarian branches. While the Christian churches are relatively familiar to most people, Elvis churches are still mostly unknown. While Christian churches obviously predate the internet by thousands of years, Elvis churches seem to have originated as a part of internet culture. While Christian churches have an internet presence that is, usually, an extension of their real world presence, Elvis churches seem to be first and foremost internet phenomena. While Christian churches almost always take their devotion to Jesus with utmost seriousness, Elvis churches are much harder to read. While some may express sincere devotion to Elvis Presley, some are decidedly tongue in cheek. And some, some are just too ambiguous to tell.

This chapter is an examination of the religious features of the internet presence of Elvis Presley. It provides a look at various websites devoted to a religious interpretation of the significance of Elvis. Some of these sites appear to be very serious, some of them appear to be intended as pure fun. All of them, as websites, are of a decidedly less than permanent nature. They may be here today, but gone tomorrow. With that in mind, I should note that this chapter constitutes a snapshot of Elvis on the internet as it appeared in the spring of 2005. Whether or not the reader will be able to find this exact information in the future is, of course, beyond my ability to tell. I would wager, however, that if the particular Elvis religious phenomena discussed here are gone, there will be plenty more to take their place.

— The Websites —

The Elvis Séance
(www.ibiblio.org/elvis/seance.html)

This website purports to be the record of a conversation
from beyond the grave with Elvis Presley. The séance
reportedly took place on the night of Elvis's birthday, January 8, 1994, and the contact with the spirit of the King
took place via a homemade Ouija board, a common device
among the spiritually inclined that is used to contact the
dead. The website lists the questions asked of the spirit and
offers both the specific responses as they appeared on the
Ouija board as well as the participants' interpretation of the
meaning of said responses. The participants asked if Elvis
was present. To this question the Ouija board answered
'yes.' The participants interpreted this to indicate that they
had successfully contacted Elvis and that Elvis was actually dead, and not just in hiding somewhere. (Reincarnation
in the form of one of the participants was ruled out because
all participants had been born prior to Elvis's death. Elvis
hiding outside the window of the room could not be ruled
out, it is noted, though the participants appear skeptical
that if the living Elvis were that close he would have
resorted to the rather inarticulate yes/no form of commu-
nication available through a Ouija board.) The spirit of Elvis
goes on to inform the participants that he approves of the
way Graceland has been operated in his absence but that
he disapproves of some of the choices made by his ex-wife
Priscilla. (One presumes that he might mean her decision
to host the *Those Amazing Animals* TV show.) He also, to
the surprise of the participants, disapproved of the Elvis
commemorative stamp.

For those who might like to try and repeat the results of
the séance the participants are kind enough to describe the

construction of the Ouija board and the specific techniques used in the ritual. The contact with Elvis, we are told, was initiated by a brief ceremony involving a lighted candle and one of the aforementioned US Postal Service stamps.

Blue Star Love (www.elvislightedcandle.org/ bluestarlove.html)

This website invites visitors to post accounts of their own spiritually significant encounters with Elvis Presley. The highlight of these postings is a transcript of telephone conversations between Elvis and Wanda June Hill, supposedly made late in Elvis's life. In these transcripts Elvis is reported to have made several significant, and startling, claims about his own spiritual nature. First of all, Elvis claims that he is 'not of this world.' While in his current state it is true that he was in human form, he claims that his true home is located near the star Rigel in the constellation Orion. His home planet has a blue sun and eight moons. Elvis's home is a mansion located beneath the shell of this planet. Elvis, in other words, claimed to be an otherworldly being whose spiritual purpose in life went far beyond the entertainment business. His mission was to spread his light to this planet, a mission that he accomplished through his dazzling talent and personal presence. Other testimonials on this website seem to support this claim that Elvis's very presence was profound enough to change lives.

Another contributor, for example, tells the story of her first attendance at an Elvis concert performance in 1969 in Las Vegas. According to this witness, what stood out most tellingly about Elvis's stage presence was his aura, that band of supernatural light, visible only to those who are spiritually receptive, which surrounds every individual to a greater or lesser extent. Elvis's aura is described as the most magnificent aura the witness has ever seen. It shaded from blue, to violet, to deep purple, with a shimmering white light encircling these inner, deeper colors. While performing, these colors would expand, sometimes rising from the top of his head, sometimes blending with the auras of band members to create a powerful light show for those with enough spiritual discernment to notice.

Another witness to Elvis's spiritual nature, identified only as Miriam, also found startling evidence of Elvis's power during one of his concert performances, which, she claims, were more religious events than simple musical shows. When Elvis performed, we are told, people screamed at his slightest movement. The air seemed to be electrified, so that his every move would send shock waves throughout the crowd. Attributing the source of Elvis's power to his 'literal magnetism' Miriam describes Elvis concerts as religious events that would draw spectators into the saving orbit of Elvis's great power. Miriam describes her own experience of the magnificence of Elvis in concert in the following way. This experience lasted

> from the anxiety and anticipation when you heard the notes of the '2001 A Space Odyssey' to the sadness and despair when the band started to play 'Can't Help Falling In Love' and you knew soon he would be gone. In between, you forgot any problems in your personal life, any hurt or disappointment, anything wrong with your health . . . anything and everything was forgotten, and everyone else ceased to exist for those 80 or so minutes. Here you were and there was Elvis . . . and life was wonderful!

In addition to providing an opportunity for fans to express their own personal testimony concerning the importance of Elvis for their lives, this website allows fans to 'light a candle for Elvis' by registering their devotion to the King. Furthermore, for those for whom a simulated candle is not enough, the site suggests other ways that a person might 'light a candle for Elvis.' These actions include being tolerant of others regardless of their ethnicity, gender, or religious beliefs, taking the time to tell someone how much you appreciate them and pointing out to them the special gifts and graces they possess which might otherwise go unnoticed, having a sense of humor in order to make others feel better, treating every human being and animal with respect, and taking time to listen to your own inner spiritual self. Carrying out these ethical and spiritual actions in your life is the best way to honor the memory of Elvis Presley, the reader is assured.

While this site does not identify itself with the concept of 'church' it does exhibit some very church-like phenomena, including testimonials concerning the object of devotion and ethical and spiritual injunctions concerning how to best represent Elvis in the world. Likewise, this list of rather straightforward, dare I say, reasonable, injunctions leads me to suspect that this website is, for the most part, to be taken seriously. One gets the feeling that the people who support this site, and who have made their testimonies public here, have done so out of a genuine sense of devotion to Elvis.

The Eighth Day Transfigurist Cult (www.ibiblio.org/elvis/cult.html)

A third site identifies itself, not as an expression of a church, but rather of a cult, and though Elvis does play a role in the beliefs expressed on this site, this role is somewhat marginal. Elvis, at least based on the content of this website, appears to be something of an afterthought in the doctrine of the Transfigurist Cult. According to this site, the Eighth Day Tranfigurists regard every eighth day as the Sabbath. They reject Leninism and Stalinism, but do not let their rejection of this political movement destroy their devotion to the color red, which is, according to their doctrine, the primary color, the color of blood. More than anything else, the Transfigurists claim that they hate hating. As a symptom of their rejection of hatred, music dwells in their hearts, and, consequently, the King of Rock 'n' Roll 'dwells in their house.' According to their testimony, 'We have seen Elvis.'

Dizgraceland Chapel (www.nwlink.com/~timelvis/chapel.html)

This site is short on written details but long on visuals. It offers visitors to the site a virtual chapel devoted to Elvis. The chapel is adorned with stained-glass windows depicting a golden-attired Elvis resting on a throne under a sparkling crown and the ceiling of the chapel depicts Elvis's head superimposed on that of God in Michelangelo's Sistine Chapel *Creation*. Apparently the religiously evocative images are meant to stand on their own without words of explanation, perhaps so that the chapel will have appeal to a larger and more diverse group of people. I imagine that a sincere Elvis devotee would find just as much pleasure here as would someone looking for an ironic laugh.

The Church of Elvis, Universal Life Church (www.compuchurch.com/coe.htm)

According to this website, the Universal Life Church, of Modesto, California, made Elvis's sainthood official on November 8, 1988. Elvis Aron Presley is thereafter to be known as Saint Elvis. The official proclamation recognizes that this honor was duly conferred upon Elvis following a petition that affirmed that as a child Elvis exhibited faith and hope when he pursued his dreams of becoming an entertainer despite overwhelming odds against his success. Furthermore, throughout his life, but especially after he had achieved great financial success, Elvis exhibited charity and generosity of spirit. These virtues of faith, hope, and charity, the petition claims, are believed by the followers of Elvis to have been present in him to an extraordinary degree.

As significant as all of this sounds, it would probably be wise not be too impressed by this announcement, however, as it appears to be quite easy to be so canonized, at least if the website's own description of the process is accurate. Visitors to the website who know of someone who has exercised the three theological virtues of faith, hope, and charity to an extraordinary degree are invited to have sainthood bestowed upon such a person by writing down the reasons someone should be so esteemed and sending it, along with a $5 donation, to the church. In addition to being so noted on the website, a Certificate of Sainthood will be sent to either the recipient of sainthood or the one making the donation. One imagines, therefore, that Elvis was canonized in exchange for a small fee, perhaps even less than $5, considering that the proclamation was made in 1988 and inflation being what it is. The ease of canonization may seem a little odd, but with fees that small we are hardly talking about the sale of indulgences.

In addition, this site claims that the Church of Elvis, a recognized sect of the Universal Life Church, has also proclaimed a special holy day in Elvis's honor. An Ecclesiastical Proclamation by a bishop of the church has declared the Saturday before Easter to be observed as Elvis Saturday and that it should 'be celebrated by the faithful in joyous recognition of all Spring Festivals associated with rebirth and fertility with the eternal melodies of St. Elvis Aron Presley, who lives forever in the eternal present.' Since Friday and Sunday seem to be taken (Good Friday and Easter) the Saturday in between seems like a perfect time to listen to Elvis songs and remember the (other) King.

For those who agree with these sentiments, there is even an opportunity to become an official representative of the church. The Universal Life Church, and its sectarian branch, the Church of Elvis, would love to attract new believers into the ordained ministry. The Universal Life Church promises to ordain anyone, for life, with no questions asked, and at no cost. This ordination is advertised as legally valid and suitable to qualify the recipient to perform weddings, funerals, and baptisms. The church imposes no doctrinal standards on its ministers or its congregations.

The First Church of Jesus Christ, Elvis (www.jubal.westnet.com/hyperdiscordia/ sacred_heart_elvis.html)

Like the Universal Life Church's Elvis sect, this site purports to represent organized groups involved in the worship of Elvis Presley. This site is distinguished by Elvis religious icons, including a picture of Elvis in the pose of Jesus of the Sacred Heart and a picture of Elvis burdened under a heavy cross. In addition, this site presents an Elvis interpretation of the Christian Gospel story in which Elvis is presented as the 'Lord of Hostess.' In this version of the Gospel, Elvis stops a mob of critics from berating a recording artist by saying 'Let him who is without bad singles cast the first rhinestone.' Likewise, this take on John 3:16 is offered: 'Elvis so loved the world that he died, fat and bloated, in a bathroom. He very pointedly did not rise from the dead three days later, but was nonetheless seen across the world by various and sundry housewives.'

In addition to attributing Christ-like qualities to Elvis, the Church of Jesus Christ, Elvis also attributes Elvis-like qualities to Jesus. In a truly inspired twist, Jesus' face is superimposed on the body of Elvis in the pose of the Elvis postage stamp. The lyrics of 'Hound Dog' are also tweaked to make the song a better fit for Jesus of Nazareth and his message. 'You ain't nothin' but a human, sinning all the time.'

Elvis Underground (www.elvisunderground.org/index2.shtml)

The Elvis Underground website includes a list of the organization's beliefs. Elvis, their doctrine claims, is the 'most fundamental material' in the universe. Like Hinduism's Brahman, or perhaps the Force of Star Wars, Elvis is the foundation of all reality, the fiber that binds the universe, and the catalyst of all movement. Elvis is the unmoved mover, the first cause of all that is. Elvis is all good and loving, and therefore so is the universe. When humans live in harmony with one another and with the universe, we are 'cousins' to Elvis. In contrast, separation from Elvis is the cause of all pain and suffering. By following the path of Elvis, 'El Camino Real' or the 'King's Highway', humans can regain balance and harmony with the universe. This state of grace is known as, of course, 'Graceland'. This path, which is followed by Elvis Underground: The church! is the path of

1 community with all things, living and non-living,
2 sustainability in regards to all facets of the environment,
3 the development and support of living networks,
4 diversity,
5 interdependence, and
6 evolution to better states of being, both conscious evolution and the evolution of consciousness.

The Church of the Militant Elvis Party (www.theplace4.co.uk/elvisseeninbaghdad/ index.htm)

Despite its name, this website is more political than it is religious. Elvis, according to church doctrine, is 'a sixty year old left wing revolutionary committed to overthrowing the capitalist system.' His motivation for his revolutionary activities may be complex, but one obvious reason is that it was the powers of capitalism that turned him into a 'fat media joke.' Following the American invasion of Iraq, the church holds that Elvis carried out his counter-capitalism activities in the heart of Baghdad. In response to an Elvis sighting in Baghdad, the church prepared a letter for President George W. Bush.

Dear George,

According to one of our missionaries, Elvis has been spotted in Baghdad. Our missionary reports that Presley was extremely angry as he had just been missed by one of your bombs in the No-Fly Zone. Our missionary further reports that Presley made this chilling prediction; 'Tell that teetotalitarian tyrant Beelzebush & his butt-sniffing buddy Tony the Lionfart that if anything happens to me during the coming offensive the Southern States will rise up under a big fan of mine Bill Clinton & start a new Civil War. Adolf Hitler fought a war on two fronts & all sane people know what happened to him & his associates.' According to our missionary Presley then disappeared into a shady night-club where he is acting as a part-time human shield for a trio of local belly-dancers.

The First Presleyterian Church of Elvis the Divine
(www.geocities.com/presleyterian_church/)

Far and away the most detailed presentation of the religious significance of Elvis Presley is found on the website of the First Presleyterian Church of Elvis the Divine, Australia. According to the official history, the church was founded in 1998 by Minister Anna. Though Anna had long been a fan of Elvis Presley, it was not until this time that she came to fully understand his religious and spiritual significance. Traveling from her native Australia to America, Anna met the mysterious Reverend Frandu and Dr. Edwards who opened her mind and heart to the truth about Elvis. According to the teachings of Frandu and Edwards, Anna learned that Presleyterians should face Las Vegas daily and make a pilgrimage to Graceland at least once during their lives. Followers are also required to maintain a well-stocked pantry containing the thirty-one items Elvis kept at Graceland, just in case Elvis happens to stop by unannounced and you need to whip up a batch of banana pudding. Presleyterians, like Elvis, are required to overindulge in the pleasures of the world. Elvis, we are told, wants us all to overindulge, at mealtime and in every way, including indulgence in 'the most glorious and divine pleasures of rock 'n' roll, extravagant outfits with capes, giant sunglasses, classic cars.' Presleyterians celebrate the holy day of Twinity, January 8, as the birthday of Elvis Aron and of his twin brother Jesse Garon. Celebrations for Twinity begin a full month ahead of time, on December 8 so that there is enough time to fit in all the parties and to participate in the most indulgent behavior possible.

> The holiday season is a time for non-stop parties, for eating and drinking too much and buying gifts for people we hardly know. It's a time for total over-indulgence. For

getting drunk. For staying up all night and sleeping in all day. For attempting to consume our entire list of 31 Holy Items in record time.

Presleyterian worship is also explained on this website. It includes congregational singing of such hymns as 'Hound Dog' and 'American Trilogy', and a sermon by Minister Anna that describes her own journey from a lost and spiritually empty sinner to someone saved by the love of Elvis. More than a testimony, this sermon is a call for listeners to accept the truth of Elvis as well.

> [D]eep down, you've always believed in the resurrection of Elvis. You've seen the 1968 Comeback Special, how much more proof do you need that Elvis was divine? In your hearts, you know Elvis was the King. And you know also that you must renounce false gods like Celine Dion, and Madonna and most of all Michael Jackson, the Anti-Elvis.

Listeners are encouraged to open their hearts to the truth of Elvis, 'to be something more than a hound dog, to finally catch a rabbit and be a friend of His.'

For those who fear that their devotion to Elvis will be mocked by their family and friends, the church offers advice. When a Christian zealot accuses a Presleyterian of being a sinner who must repent, the Presleyterian is to remind them that Elvis worship is about 'food, fun, and frolic' and that it rejects guilt and damnation. To those who claim Elvis was only a man, now deceased, the Presleyterian must remind them that Elvis has transcended the flesh to become a being of flesh and spirit. He can materialize and dematerialize at will. In no case should a follower of Elvis grow worried or afraid, for Elvis will surely give him or her the words to say. 'Just be steadfast in your belief in Elvis and He will fill your mouth with words the way He filled His mouth with peanut-butter-and-banana sandwiches.'

Presleyterian religion is not all hymn singing and partying, however, for church members are also encouraged to become very involved in church-supported political initiatives. These political initiatives include

1 federal funding for the 'Big Breakfasts for School-kids Program' to ensure that children get their required six meals a day,
2 involuntary prayer in school to reverse the dangerous trend away from Elvis worship in the public schools,
3 putting the E into ecology and powering our technology with the power of Elvis,
4 Elvis-style healthcare reform that includes support of the Elvis diet plan guaranteed to make people immortal, like Elvis, and
5 Elvis work projects to include putting unemployed people to work building shrines to Elvis in every community in the nation.

— Sincerity and Irony, With and Without a Cause —

What this survey of internet websites devoted to Elvis and religion demonstrates, first of all, is that there is a diversity of ways in which Elvis's religious significance can be approached. First, there are clearly examples of websites that take Elvis's religious significance very seriously. While some of these focus on Elvis as a Christian role model and on his gospel music, and others point toward Elvis's later infatuation with new age spirituality, those that concern us here are those that attribute religious meaning to Elvis himself. This sincere approach to Elvis and religion is seen most clearly perhaps in the site devoted to Elvis's Blue Star Love. Here, it seems to me, we are clearly dealing with motivations rooted in sincere devotion to Elvis as a supernatural figure, or at least an extraterrestrial figure, whose life was a means of spreading the spiritual truth.

Other websites that seem to be sincere in their Elvis devotion, but whose motivation does not appear as certain to me include the sites devoted to the Elvis séance, the Eighth Day Transfigurist Cult, the Church of Elvis–Universal Life Church, and Elvis Underground. These sites appear to be sincere in their association of religious imagery with Elvis, but the nature of irony is, of course, such that one is never sure. Both the Elvis séance and the Eighth Day Transfigurist Cult appear sincere simply because the claims that are made by each of them are so minimalist. The participants in the Elvis séance claim to have contacted Elvis from beyond the dead, but he really says little of interest. Elvis is, here, nothing more than the particular person the group decided to contact as part of the practicing of a relatively non-Elvis related religious ritual. The Transfigurist Cult likewise attaches only minimal religious significance to Elvis. Though I confess that I have a very difficult time understanding the nature of the beliefs being espoused on this site, I see no reason to suspect that they are less than sincere and that their inclusion of Elvis is anything other than an expression of some sort of Elvis devotion. The same holds for the Church of Elvis branch of the Universal Life Church. Since practically anyone is a potential candidate for sanctification, the fact that Elvis is regarded as a saint seems to be of little consequence. I suspect that there may be sincere respect for Elvis at play here, but I have no reason to believe that it rises to the level of a cult or new religious movement.

The Elvis Underground site, on the other hand, is a bit more problematic. For while some of the claims seem to be made almost tongue in cheek the overall emphasis of the site seems to be rather sincere. In other words, it seems that while some rather absurd claims about Elvis as the glue that holds the universe together might lead you to suspect that your leg is being pulled, the actual ethical and political causes of this group seem to be very serious. It almost looks as if the elements of Elvis devotion have been added on as an afterthought, as there is no attempt to establish a connection between the beliefs about Elvis and the ethical-political claims of the group. I am tempted to say that Elvis Underground stands as a sort of border case between websites that express a sincere devotion to Elvis, and websites that approach Elvis and religion more ironically, especially if we recognize that some uses of irony are at the service of very sincere motivations and goals. Such a mixture of irony and sincerity comprises the second type of website that we have examined.

The second category of website that we have encountered includes those which take an ironic approach to Elvis and religion, but do so for very sincere reasons. If the Elvis Underground is a borderline case of this type, then the Church of the Militant Elvis Party is a much more straightforward case of the same. Here, an obviously ironic attitude toward Elvis is used in the service of rather serious anti-imperialist political objectives.

A third category of website that features religious interpretations of Elvis Presley is composed of those that are, in my reading, entirely ironic in nature. These sites include the First Church of Jesus Christ, Elvis and the First Presleyterian Church of Elvis the Divine. Here the webmasters are obviously engaged is some serious pranking, though the Presleyterian site in particular goes so far in its joke that it might be easy to be persuaded, if one is not careful, that such is meant to be taken seriously. (Well, of course, it is meant to be taken seriously, though only by those on the outside of the joke.) Ironically, I suppose we should say, the First Presleyterian Church of Elvis the Divine, like the Twenty-Four Hour Church of Elvis, are often cited as examples by those wishing to establish the hypothesis that Elvism is sure to be the next big religion.

Finally, there are some websites that I have to say are just too close to call. I can't tell whether or not the creators are sincere or ironic. Your guess is as good as mine concerning the Dizgraceland Chapel. Though considering the name, I strongly suspect someone thinks it is pretty funny.

— Conclusion —

Once again, it seems irony gets in the way of the Elvis devotion that I have been looking for. What, with the Twenty-Four Hour Church of Elvis not being a church but rather some sort of ironic bit of outsider performance art, and the First Presleyterian Church of Elvis the Divine looking more like some elaborate joke than like a sincere example of Elvis devotion, one might begin to wonder if there is much to be said about Elvis and religion that does not fall into the category of some sort of pop cultural construct. Having failed to find a religious cult centered around Graceland or an order of priests comprised of Elvis impersonators, it seems that the religious significance of Elvis Presley is something that has, for the most part, been explored by Hollywood filmmakers, novelists, songwriters, artists, and internet comedians. Some have, no doubt, been sincere in their exploration and interpretation of Elvis's religious significance and I think that much of what they have to say is important and profound. (I confess, more important and profound than anything I thought I was going to discover when I started on this journey.) As important and profound as it may be, however, such artistic exploration and expression does not constitute the sincere, serious, deeply felt devotion that I discovered in a woman late one night in a Memphis emergency room.

There are hints of such devotion in the sincere admiration with which many Elvis fans regard the King, as well as in the deep respect shown to Elvis by most tribute artists. It also appears in the fictional writings and artistic creations of a few fans, as well as in the frenzied obsession of, say, Paul MacLeod and Joni Mabe. Likewise, as we have seen in this chapter, it appears in the vaguest of ways on the internet, though it is there almost entirely obscured by the ironists.

My journey is not quite at an end, however, not when as I check out at the local grocery store, those tabloid headlines keep jumping out at me . . .

8

Elvis in the Tabloids
Alive and Coming Back!

Elvis Presley enjoyed a place in tabloid newspapers long before he died. His affairs with his leading ladies, his engagement and marriage to Priscilla, and the ups and downs of his career all served to intrigue supermarket shoppers and hence sell newspapers. After his death, however, Elvis's place in tabloid journalism would rise to an unrivaled position. In the pages of such newspapers, and on gossipy and sensationalistic television programs, stories claiming that Elvis's death was faked were reinforced by eyewitness reports of people who claimed to have seen Elvis alive and well, years after his supposed 'death.' Alongside UFOs, Bigfoot, the Loch Ness Monster, JFK, and astronomical and psychic predictions, Elvis is a staple of supermarket tabloid headlines.

Elvis: The Untold Story
The Last Picture
(*National Enquirer*, 16 August 1978)

Elvis!
What this Psychic Found at the King's Secret Love Nest
in Desert
(*Midnight Globe*, 11 September 1979)

> Statue of Elvis Found on Mars:
> Satellite Beams Back 'All Shook Up'
> (*Sun* (US), 20 September 1988)
>
> Elvis Seen at Graceland!
> He's in a wheelchair, but The King is back . . .
> (*Weekly World News*, 1 October 2003)

— Orion —

The person most responsible for the development of a conspiracy theory around the death of Elvis Presley, and hence for the proliferation of tabloid headlines about such a conspiracy, is Gail Brewer-Giorgio. According to Brewer-Giorgio, immediately after hearing of the death of Elvis Presley, she was inspired to write a fictional novel about a character she called Orion, a southerner of humble origins who rises to superstar status and then fakes his own death to escape the price of fame. This novel, *Orion: The Living Superstar of Song*, described how a wax dummy of Orion was placed in a coffin and buried and how Orion and his family escaped into the night with new identities and freedom from the prison of their fame. In Brewer-Giorgio's account, the publication of her novel was followed by very strange events.

First, her novel was inexplicably recalled by her publisher, and copies were pulled from the shelf, perhaps, Brewer-Giorgio surmises, because it was discovered by those in the know that her fictional story had inadvertently contained the truth about the 'death' of Elvis. In addition to this, Brewer-Giorgio claims she soon discovered that Sun Records was using characters from her novel without having received her permission to do so. The singer Jimmy Ellis had caused a stir earlier when his voice, which sounded uncannily like that of Elvis, had been dubbed onto a track by Jerry Lee Lewis and identified simply as 'a friend.' Speculation ran high that this was either an old recording of Elvis and Lewis, or more tantalizing, a new recording proving that Elvis was still alive. Now, Sun Records had taken Ellis and given him an Elvis haircut and jumpsuit and covered his face with a lone-ranger mask. He was dubbed 'Orion' and his first Sun Records release, *Reborn*, featured a drawing of an empty casket on the front cover, clearly meant to evoke an image of Elvis returned from the grave.

Brewer-Giorgio claimed she had no connection whatsoever to Sun Records or Jimmy Ellis as Orion. The mystery deepened for her, she asserts, when witnesses reported that they had seen *two* men dressed as Orion. Brewer-Giorgio wonders, could there be two Orions, one Jimmy Ellis and the other Elvis himself? Could her fictional novel have given Elvis an opportunity to continue performing and recording as Orion? What better way to hide than in plain sight as an Elvis impersonator? Convinced that her book was prophetic and that something very similar really did happen to Elvis, Brewer-Giorgio began a search for clues. The clues she unearthed constitute the main form of evidence usually mentioned in tabloid articles in support of the belief that Elvis did not die in August of 1977 and that he is still alive today.

— Is Elvis Alive? —

With her novel pulled off the shelves, Brewer-Giorgio next published a far more successful second book, a nonfiction account of the publication of *Orion* and of the startling discoveries she had made. *Is Elvis Alive?*, along with the subsequent *The Elvis Files: Was His Death Faked?*, and *Elvis Undercover: Is He Alive and Coming Back?* offer Brewer-Giorgio's assessment of the evidence in support of the Orion hypothesis, the hypothesis that Elvis faked his own death. The following are a sampling of the kinds of claims that Brewer-Giorgio makes in support of her hypothesis.

1 Elvis was a drug enforcement agent and may have been placed in the witness protection program or gone deep undercover. It is public knowledge that he had met with President Nixon to discuss assisting with drug enforcement and that he had received a DEA badge. He may have even had an undercover drug agent working with his band. Is it possible that Elvis had a deeper involvement in undercover work than we know? Did something go wrong and force Elvis to have to change his identity for his own protection, or is it possible that he sought to change his identity so that he could go undercover on his own?

2 Elvis's middle name is misspelled on his gravestone as 'Aaron', rather than as 'Aron'. The 'Aron' spelling was significant to Elvis and his family and the gravestone is the only place where this mistake was made. Is it possible that a superstitious Elvis saw misspelling his name on the phony grave stone as way to ward off bad luck?

3 The novel *The Passover Plot*, which describes how Jesus and his disciples faked his death and resurrection, was found at Graceland after Elvis 'died.' Could this be a clue left by the King? Did reading this book give him the idea? Did he leave it in plain view as a clue to friends, family, and fans?

4 Mysterious recordings by someone identified as Sivle Nora (Elvis Aron in reverse) and shared with Brewer-Giorgio may be recordings by Elvis himself, meant to be recognized only by the faithful.

5 Photographs have been taken of Elvis after the time of his supposed death, including a picture of Elvis looking out of the pool house door at Graceland and a picture of Elvis with Jesse Jackson and Muhammad Ali. The pool house photo prompted Graceland to install a solid door so that tourists are no longer

able to see inside the building. Muhammad Ali, though asked many times about the photo with Elvis, has never clearly denied that it was the King.

6   Elvis's death certificate lists his weight as 170 pounds, though he clearly weighed much more than that in August of 1977. Why this discrepancy if his body had actually been examined by a coroner?

7   No one has claimed Elvis's life insurance policy.

8   Witnesses described the body in the casket as being 'wax-like' with a pug nose. Elvis's nose was anything but 'pug'. The hands were also said to be soft and pudgy, while Elvis's hands were strong and calloused due to his karate practice.

9   Elvis is not buried next to his mother as he clearly expressed his desire to be. Instead he is between his father and grandmother. If Elvis is really in the grave, why weren't his wishes honored? Is it possible that the place of honor next to his mother still awaits him?

10   Pallbearers report that the coffin was extremely heavy with cool air seeping out. This might indicate the presence of an air-conditioner unit in the coffin to keep the wax dummy from melting. A specialized coffin such as this would have to have been ordered months in advance, indicating that Elvis had been plotting his 'death' for some time.

Brewer-Giorgio's books offer countless other bits of evidence of just this sort to confirm her hypothesis that Elvis faked his death in a way suspiciously similar to that found in her novel *Orion*. In addition she offers interviews with close associates of Elvis, who she believes offer confirmatory testimony. For example, she records the following exchange with Elvis's cousin, Gene Smith in *The Elvis Files*.

'I saw Elvis a few weeks before August 16', said Gene. 'He told me, "Gene, I envy you. You can go anywhere. If you want to stop someplace for a beer, you can. I'm living the most miserable son-of-a-bitchin' life anyone could live!" Elvis also told me,' he continued, 'shortly before the sixteenth, that he would be going away for a while, but that he would contact me later.' Then, when Gene heard Elvis had died, he said he couldn't believe it, felt something was wrong – and then *knew* something was wrong when he went to the viewing.

'The first thing I saw when I went to the coffin', Gene related, 'was the hands. They weren't Elvis's. You see, Elvis's hands were big and beat up – calluses on the knuckles, scars, a crooked finger – all this from karate, breaking boards, smashing bricks. The hands in the coffin were small and smooth as a woman's, smooth as a baby's behind. They were definitely not Elvis's. Plus, the sideburns were glued on; one was sticking straight out at the side. When I noticed this, some man came over and patted it back down, like he was sticking it back on. The nose was all wrong – pugged. Elvis had a straight nose. The eyebrows were wrong, the forehead wrong, hairline wrong. I could even see where the hair had been glued on around the forehead – you could see the glue.'

'Could it have been a wax dummy?' I asked Gene.

'Could have been', Gene responded. '*I* thought it was.'

'Many who viewed the body in the coffin noted what they termed as "beads of sweat"', I told him.

'That's true', Gene answered. 'I saw it, too.'

Laughingly, I reminded Gene that dead bodies don't sweat. He said, 'I know. Plus,' he added, 'if it was a wax dummy, then there had to have been an air conditioner in the coffin. I think there might have been. I was one of the ten pallbearers, and that coffin was so heavy I fell to my knees. The coffin was *too* heavy to have had just a body in it.'

'One of Elvis's friends', I added, 'said the same thing, that he knew it was not Elvis in the coffin, and asked Vernon Presley what was going on, where Elvis *was*. Vernon told him that Elvis was *upstairs* . . .' (Brewer-Giorgio 1990: 240–241)

The rest of Brewer-Giorgio's writing follows this same style. If there is so much smoke, she seems to say, there must be a fire. Of course the kind of evidence that one might most want to have would be actual proof that Elvis is alive today and not just theories to explain strange testimonies about his death and burial. Brewer-Giorgio does not disappoint in this regard and offers in *The Elvis Files* what she calls 'A Potpourri of Alleged Contacts with Elvis' (167).

— Elvis Sightings —

According to Brewer-Giorgio, following the publication of *Is Elvis Alive?*, she received many letters from individuals who recounted their encounters with someone who looked like, or even claimed to be, the supposedly deceased entertainer. Brewer-Giorgio protects the identity of her sources by not printing any last names. This is done, she claims, because of the negative publicity that surrounded the testimony of Louise Welling of Kalamazoo, Michigan, who claimed to see Elvis in her city. People like Welling, according to Brewer-Giorgio, find themselves in a dilemma. The media wants to know why more people don't come forward to confirm that Elvis is alive. Yet, when they do come forward, the media treats them as if the were 'wackos' (Brewer-Giorgio 1998: 168). Hence the need for privacy and anonymity.

Some of Brewer-Giorgio's sighting are hardly worthy of the name, however, and should give the witnesses little reason to worry about media persecution. For example, Brewer-Giorgio prints a letter from 'Bill A. of Orange, California' written in the late 1980s but retelling an event from 1979. Bill A. was not himself the witness, but heard the story from a friend. This unnamed friend had placed an ad in southern California newspapers in an attempt to sell a 1976 Bicentennial Edition Harley-Davidson motorcycle. The friend was soon contacted by a man who identified himself as a representative of George Barris, a well-known

Hollywood car designer. When Barris arrived to take a look at the bike, he told the friend that he was a close friend of Elvis and that he knew for a fact Elvis was still alive (169– 170). Brewer-Giorgio, in other words, offers a letter from 'Bill A.', which recounts a story he heard from a friend to the effect that George Barris claimed that Elvis is alive. Not exactly a sighting.

A little less ambiguous is an account that Brewer-Giorgio publishes alongside the previous one. This story is from 'Alton R.' from Nashville, Tennessee, who was working at a gas station when he saw the King. Alton reports that around 9:30 p.m., while Alton was talking to his mother on the telephone, a man stopped and filled up his car with gas. As the man walked toward the store, Alton told his mother that he thought the man was Elvis Presley. The man paid with a credit card, but did not speak, even when Alton told him that he thought that he looked like Elvis. Alton then noticed his gold jewelry and the gold $20-piece belt buckle and remarked about them. Still no response. As the man left, Alton asked once more. This time he got a response: a crooked smile and a wink (170).

Ripped right from the headlines of tabloid newspapers and considerably padding out Brewer-Giorgio's list of sightings is Peter Eicher's *The Elvis Sightings*. Eicher, like Brewer-Giorgio, describes Elvis sightings by people given only a first name, to protect them from the media. Eicher's introduction says all we need to know about the kind of stories we will be given and about the tabloid quality of reporting with which his book is filled. His book, he writes, contains no proof that Elvis is alive. However, it also contains no proof that Elvis is dead. He has no completely verified stories of people having seen Elvis. But he also has no complete verification that they didn't. Indeed, Eicher's take on the testimony of his subjects places Elvis sightings as much in the category of faith as fact. The stories of Elvis sightings that he reports are true to the people who reported them, he claims. Some of them may have doubts, but most have unshakable faith that Elvis is alive (Eicher 1993: 5–6).

Much more so than Brewer-Giorgio's reports of sightings, those collected in *The Elvis Sightings* take on an ethical or religious quality. I am reminded of the sightings of Jesus by his disciples after his death. Elvis is presented as 'spreading the gospel' of his music, by giving a young heavy-metal fan in a laundromat a cassette tape of one of his live performances and by appearing on stage in a Louisiana bar to perform his old songs once again. In an appearance to a man on the Appalachian Trail, Elvis even launched into a full-scale discourse on God, human suffering, and the afterlife. Speaking in religious imagery, Elvis described the faking of his death and his escape from his fame. He had simply made a decision to follow the light and to escape from the darkness that had overtaken his life (121).

In another instance, Elvis's advice to a suicidal young man named 'Dog' at the Gateway Arch in St. Louis turns the man's life around.

> 'Know what Elvis? When I walk under that arch, nothing's going to be the same anymore. It's the gateway to everything. It'll all be different.'
>
> 'You think so, Dog?'
>
> 'Yeah, I know so . . . John.' An edge of doubt crept back into Dog's voice.
>
> 'John? Why are you calling me John?'
>
> 'Because that's your name. C'mon, you're not really Elvis. Elvis is dead.'
>
> 'Maybe he is and maybe he isn't', Elvis said. 'There are other gateways in this world, Dog, gateways not many people know about.' (89)

While Gail Brewer-Giorgio appealed to Elvis sightings as a way to establish her thesis that Elvis was not really dead, the sightings as told by Peter Eicher are presented as that and as something more. While some of them are pedestrian and earthbound, others take on the quality of religious visions and of life-changing experiences. They are less about the establishment of the fact that Elvis's death was faked and more about the nature of Elvis himself, whether his current existence is considered physical or spiritual, earthly or heavenly. To say that 'Elvis is alive' borders on a confession of faith, like saying 'Jesus is Lord,' and sightings are more like visions than like eyewitness accounts. Eicher's conclusion makes the religious aspects of the sightings clear and links Elvis's post-death appearances, and his anticipated return, with those of Jesus.

> And so the mystery stands. Very little is clear, very little is certain, but between the fateful day of August 16, 1977 and the present lies a great, dark cloud of doubt and wonder. A few shafts of light have pierced that cloud, and a shadowy figure has been seen within, but the cloud always draws itself closed and the figure disappears again into the mists. We cannot understand why he chooses to remain secluded; we don't know when the clouds will part, but we will dare to say this: The King lives. And someday the King will return.
>
> Until then, we have a thousand songs to warm our hearts and a million memories to dry our tears. Where there was once only the sadness of death, now we have the joy of hope, the felicity of possibility. We can do nothing but wait, so wait we shall, for the day when the dark clouds will part and the world will once again greet its great son, the man, the mystery, the forever King of Rock and Roll, Elvis Aron Presley. (209)

Of course, we might want to ask about Eicher's motivations. Is his work a sincere testimonial to his belief that Elvis is alive and coming back or is it meant as an ironic joke, or even worse, a crass attempt to appeal to the emotions of fans in order to sell books? The tabloid-style journalism of both Brewer-Giorgio and Eicher lend themselves to any of these interpretations. Tabloid newspapers, themselves, notoriously walk a fine line between journalism and outright fiction. (Some, like the wonderful *Weekly World News* embrace the fictional with such gusto that only a fool would take it as fact. 'Batboy Led Our Troops to Sadaam's Hole', indeed.) Either way, it is certain that many who read Eicher's account will read it as an example of the former, rather than the latter. In other words, regardless of Eicher's motivations, many readers will undoubtedly take the work at face value, as an account of the many Elvis sightings that have occurred since his death and as an expression of Eicher's personal faith in the life and eminent return of Elvis.

— The Return of the King —

The question of whether or not such tabloid-ready material is the authentic expression of an author's beliefs or an ironic or commercial 'put-on' is also unavoidable when considering Jay Gould's pronouncements concerning Elvis. Gould, who claims to be a psychic consulted by Elvis many times before his death, makes a claim for his book *Elvis 2000: The King Returns* that would make any tabloid newspaper editor sit up and take notice. This book, according to Gould, consists of a series of communications delivered by Elvis to the psychic from beyond the grave. In the author's note Gould declares that he had been in contact with Elvis more than forty times since his death. It is reported that Elvis communicated to Gould in a special code, which had then been translated into English. The code dictations, he claims, 'are the exclusive property of the Church of Elvis, and will only be revealed after his return in August 2000.'

Elvis religion

In the course of these 'forty or more' psychic visitations Elvis revealed to Gould many things about his spiritual nature and purpose. He had always known that he was a prophet, destined, like Jesus, to redeem the world. His suffering and death only served to prepare him for his final act of redemption. According to Elvis's spiritual testimony,

> Scrawled across the Wall of Love at Graceland is an immense scripture written from the heart. You could call it the Bible of the Church of Elvis Presley. The names on that wall endlessly erased to make space for new inscriptions are the names of those who will be gathered together on my return. The huge festival thrown in my honor, at which I will perform a new set of songs with the Band of Angels will also involve my healing the sick amongst my followers. . . . The King will personally redeem the poor and the suffering. The Earth is about to encounter the infiltration of Elvites. The latter are a species of aliens who work in my name. (Gould 2000: 21–22)

In preparation for the second coming of King Elvis, his followers should go into the desert in groups, meditate with the mantra 'E,' and light candles in Elvis's name.

In addition to the promise of his second coming, Elvis reveals that there is life on Mars, that he has recorded new music with such deceased luminaries as John Lennon and Jimi Hendrix, that he has met and knows the identity of Jack the Ripper, that Hitler escaped the earth in a flying saucer, and that Elvis had an affair with Jackie Kennedy. He shares recipes for Martian Red Ice Cream, Roast Peacock, Mojo Burgers (a King-size burger in the shape of a piano with the lid open), and other newly discovered delectables. He also provides his followers with instructions concerning how to contact him in the intervening time, a process that Elvis claims is 'as easy as operating a website.' First, one should sit in a quiet, dark place. Second, light a candle and place it in front of a photograph of Elvis. Third, close your eyes and prepare to meditate. Fourth, 'mentally type a code into your mind. The code you need to access me is 56565616. Repeat that number three times in your head.' Fifth, the angelic presence of Elvis will appear, surrounded by light. Sixth, if Elvis does not appear, use the mantra 'EP' as a focus of meditation. Seventh, 'Keep me near you for so long as you wish' (57–59).

Even more so than with Eicher's book, it seems clear that if *Elvis 2000* is not an outright spoof, then it is certainly a crass attempt to make money from gullible, tabloid-reading, consumers. Furthermore, unlike Eicher's book, it seems unlikely, considering the nature of the claims, to have been convincing to any readers, even those who read it prior to the day of Elvis's scheduled return in August, 2000. If it is meant as such a spoof, however, it is a brilliant one. Gould offers no clues, at least discernible to this author, that give it away. Unlike *Templars of the Christian Brotherhood*, by David Paul and Geoffrey Todd, which clearly identifies itself as a work of fiction and is treated as such in this book along with other Elvis fiction, Gould's *Elvis 2000* refuses to give up the joke.

— The Elvis–Jesus Mystery —

An even odder and more inexplicable work than Gould's is Cinda Godfrey's *The Elvis–Jesus Mystery: The Shocking Scriptural and Scientific Evidence that Elvis Presley Could Be the Messiah Anticipated throughout History*. After the title itself, the next clue to the reader that they are in unusual territory is found on the acknowledgements page. Godfrey writes:

> It is customary for an author to thank all those persons who supported and encouraged her in the writing of a given book.

Unfortunately, due to the subject matter of this particular (and peculiar) book, I racked my brain but could think of no one who supported me or encouraged me throughout this endeavor. In fact, my family ran like rats on a sinking ship and my passion for the subject of my manuscript actually estranged me from those I love. It's been a long, lonely road to hoe. (Godfrey 1999)

The peculiar and controversial nature of her book is a result of Godfrey's combination of elements from Brewer-Giorgio's Orion hypothesis, various 'new age' epistemological techniques, and the interpretation of Biblical prophecy as practiced by extreme forms of Christian evangelism. It is also this combination that makes the work not only peculiar and controversial but of great interest to anyone engaged in a study of the religious aspects of the Elvis phenomenon. Brewer-Giorgio's tabloid-style conspiracy theory and the 'Jesus-like' posthumous Elvis sightings of Brewer-Giorgio and Eicher come to full religious expression in Godfrey's writing. She takes tabloid Elvis journalism, mixes it with Christian prophecy and new age spirituality, and transforms it into Elvis religion. Whether or not Godfrey writes from authentic belief in her claims or ironically is difficult to ascertain, though I for one am persuaded that Godfrey does believe what she writes. If not, and I end up with egg on my face for believing she is sincere, I won't be the first person fooled by a good tabloid-style hoax.

Adam/Jesus (Elvis)

Godfrey claims that her religious interest in Elvis Presley arose as the result of watching an interview with Gail Brewer-Giorgio on Oprah Winfrey's television program in May of 1988. She found Brewer-Giorgio's claims to be quite intriguing, but as a born-again Christian since 1974 Godfrey was a little bothered by her own growing obsession with Elvis. She then began to pray to God about Elvis and was led, through correspondence with Brewer-Giorgio, to Kate McNeil of Southgate Michigan. McNeil, in a series of telephone conversations, convinced Godfrey that the answer she was seeking was right in the heart of her Christian religion. Adam, Jesus, and Elvis are one and the same person – all represented by the figure of Orion, as perceived by Brewer-Giorgio in her fictional novel.

In the Garden of Eden, Satan tricked Adam into sin. Because of God's law of retribution, Adam had to return to earth and live a sinless life as he was meant to do in the beginning. The form Adam assumed for his second coming was that of Jesus. Likewise, in order to compensate for the bringing of spiritual death to the world, Adam/Jesus had to bring spiritual life back to humanity, a task accomplished through his crucifixion. This accomplished, Adam had to return once more to retrieve the spiritual kingdom lost to Satan in Adam's fall from grace. This third incarnation was in the form of Elvis Presley. This time, however, Adam/Jesus/Elvis tricked Satan into thinking that he was dead, even hoaxing his own death to look like a drug overdose. Satan believed he had killed Elvis. Elvis, however, is far from dead (Godfrey 1999: 11).

Here we have a clear example of contemporary religious syncretism. Christian theology is combined with new age beliefs concerning reincarnation and with Brewer-Giorgio's Orion conspiracy theory. While Brewer-Giorgio only claimed that Elvis had faked his death for straightforward human reasons such as to escape his fame or to work undercover for the CIA, Godfrey connects the faked death with a much deeper theological motivation. Elvis faked his death to fool Satan and the forces of Evil. His return from hiding will therefore be to spell the defeat of Satan, the redemption of humanity, and the establishment of God's kingdom on earth.

Christian Prophecy

The influence of conservative Christian theology upon God-frey does more than provide the broad canvas upon which her story of creation, fall, and redemption takes place. In addition, her conservative Christian understanding of Biblical prophecy leads her to believe that the end times, the time of the fulfillment of prophecy and the final redemption of creation, is near. The belief that Elvis is the promised messiah is strengthened when we understand that the Bible long ago predicted that the present age would be the time for the fulfillment of prophecy. Following the interpretation of prophecy offered by Hal Lindsey, among others, Godfrey sees evidence in the political, social, ethical, and environmental state of our world that the end is near. Her litany of evidences for the state of the world is not original, but sounds much like that offered by countless fundamentalist Christian evangelists. She claims that by the year 2000 sixty per cent of all births will be illegitimate, that the one world government foretold by the prophet Daniel is rapidly becoming reality, that the last half of the twentieth century has been marked by 'increasingly violent weather patterns,' and that the Aids and Ebola viruses constitute the plagues predicted in the Bible. Furthermore, the strange lights seen in the sky and popularly called UFOs are the signs in the sky foretold by Jesus and sure signs of the end (Godfrey 1999: 15–20).

To top it all off, Godfrey presents two other claims at the centerpiece of her evidence that the end times are upon us, just as the Bible predicted. The first of these is the well-used claim made by many end-time conspiracy theorists, to the effect that the Antichrist has already established a system for placing his evil mark upon the unsuspecting masses. This mark, the notorious 666, will be placed on the back of the hand or on the forehead, and without it individuals will not be able to participate in the global economy.

Those who refuse the mark will suffer starvation and persecution. Those who take it will be marked as children of Satan.

> Now, if you think this sounds like pure science fiction, please note that, at this writing, there is an enormous computer system placed and ready for action in Luxembourg, Belgium (seat of the New World Order). This monster of a computer has the capability to track and mark every human being on the planet. Satellites orbiting the earth are already tracking our every move. Now . . . would you like to learn the *name* of this computer system? Are you ready for this? It has been dubbed the **B**elgian **E**lectronic **A**utomated **S**ystems **T**erminal! **B-E-A-S-T!** The Bible – outdated? *I don't think so!* (45–46)

In addition to this claim, proffered by the more conspiratorial-minded of Biblical fundamentalists, Godfrey offers up another bit of evidence that also has a home in more mainstream evangelical quarters: the creation of the nation of Israel in 1948 marks a central turning-point in history. This central event was prophesied by Jesus himself and was followed by his assurance that the generation that witnesses the rebirth of Israel will also witness the end of the world (17).

The interesting thing about Godfrey's interpretation of Biblical prophecy is that it is not unusual, or that far out of the evangelical Christian mainstream. Such claims are made on a regular basis by television evangelists and from church pulpits. In a similar, if not identical, form, this approach to the interpretation of prophecy is espoused by luminaries on the American Protestant scene such as Pat Robertson, former Republican Party presidential candidate. Millions of evangelical Christians would accept Godfrey's prophetic interpretations as quite orthodox.

Tabloid Conspiracy Theory

Into this matrix of Christian theology Godfrey places the tabloid-friendly conspiracy theory of Gail Brewer-Giorgio. Though Godfrey states that her intent is not to prove that Elvis faked his own death, because Brewer-Giorgio has already established that fact, she nevertheless devotes a chapter to demonstrating just such a claim. Most of what she says is clearly influenced by Brewer-Giorgio and consists of undocumented comments from family and friends about what Elvis did and said prior to his death and about the events surrounding his funeral. Likewise, most of her evidence is given in the form of questions that point the reader to what Godfrey believes is the only logical conclusion: Elvis is alive!

Why did Elvis change his will just prior to his death? Why has no one claimed his life insurance? If Elvis was so sick how could he play several hours of racquetball the evening before he died? Why did Elvis make frequent visits to the Memphis Funeral Home? Why, considering his weight gain, didn't Elvis order new jumpsuits in preparation for his upcoming concert schedule? Why did the death certificate significantly understate Elvis's death weight? Why does the photo of Elvis in his casket, published by the *National Enquirer,* look nothing like Elvis? Why was Elvis's eulogy delivered by a *comedian?* Why did Tom Parker wear a Hawaiian shirt and baseball cap to the funeral? And finally, that perpetual mystery, why is Elvis's name misspelled on his gravestone as 'Aaron' and not 'Aron?' These pointed questions are clearly the kind of questions first brought to light by Brewer-Giorgio and made famous in tabloid newspapers and television daytime talk shows throughout the 1980s. Godfrey's insistence that there is only one reasonable explanation to these questions, following the 'if there is smoke there must be a fire' argument, also mimics that of Brewer-Giorgio. Godfrey writes:

A skeptic could probably manufacture a million and one different explanations to all of these questions. But wouldn't it be smarter and far easier to just accept the singular explanation which answers all of them . . . . . .
. . . . **ELVIS PRESLEY IS ALIVE?** (Godfrey 1999: 69)

Godfrey adds to Brewer-Giorgio's argument that Elvis is alive with the inclusion of an odd story of a young girl named Renee, from Southgate, Michigan, who was visited by the angel Gabriel in 1958. (Godfrey identifies this girl using the pseudonym of 'Renee' but one can't help wonder how 'Renee' is connected to Kate McNeil, also of Southgate, Michigan, who first revealed the secret of the Elvis–Jesus mystery to Godfrey.) This story also seems to serve as the crucial link between Biblical prophecy and the faking of Elvis's death. According to Godfrey, Gabriel told Renee that he would reveal a great secret to her on the condition that she remain a virgin until she was married. Not knowing what the word 'virgin' meant, Renee was told by her mother that it meant to be 'untouched by a man.' Renee apparently took her mother literally and refused to be even touched by her male classmates after this event. The secret revealed to Renee is that Elvis would marry someone named Priscilla who would be a false bride. Elvis would then fake his death (51–52). Following this visitation, Renee was instructed to write down the revelation, seal it, date it, sign it, and have three witnesses sign it. She was then to bury it with a robin's feather. She was to tell no one of the revelation until God revealed it to the world. Renee was told that at the proper time God would reveal the burial place to a construction worker who would then sell it to the tabloids. Tabloid conspiracy theory is thus firmly linked with Christian prophecy.

The Seventh Seal

According to Godfrey, Renee's second visitation occurred in 1973 when John the Baptist appeared to her with a new revelation. He revealed to Renee that August 16, 1977 would inaugurate the beginning of God's final revelation. The mysterious seventh seal of the Book of Revelation would finally be opened just as had been described in Revelation 8:1, 'When the Lamb broke open the seventh seal, there was silence in the heaven for about half an hour.' From this point on Godfrey presents evidence after evidence that Elvis is the subject of the scroll of the seventh seal. After all, the crucial verse is Revelation *8:1*, and Elvis himself was born on *January 8*. From here on, Godfrey's case gets decidedly weirder. For example:

> Renee (who is something of a prophet in her own right) explained that God told Elvis to keep silent and not to defend himself against the charges leveled against him by his family, his associates, his critics, and the media.
> **INTERESTING! VERY INTERESTING!**
> The *'Lamb of God'* refers to the Son. The Son is Jesus. If Elvis and Jesus are the same soul, then . . . .
> ELVIS IS THE LAMB OF GOD . . . .
> AND GOD TOLD HIS LAMB TO BE SILENT . . . . . .
> **SILENCE OF THE LAMB** . . . .
> Could that be where producers got the title for the motion picture hit by the same name starring Jodie Foster? Suddenly, I remembered a photo of Elvis which appeared on the cover of a major news stand tabloid! I distinctly recalled it because, first of all, I don't buy tabloid newspapers. Most of them are trash. But this particular photo of Elvis had supposedly been snapped by a woman in **1991** as Elvis exited a movie theater in St. Louis, Missouri. . . .
> I had saved the tabloid somewhere in my Elvis collection. I began searching for it because I vaguely recalled something written on the theater marquee just behind

Elvis in the photo. I found it and **sure enough!** The photo was taken as Elvis came out of the movie, '**Silence of the Lambs**.' Now . . . . . you might not find that remarkable, but I do!

The only legitimate photo ever taken of Elvis since his 1977 disappearance (death) and directly behind him is a sign which reads 'SILENCE OF THE LAMBS'!

'When the **Lamb** broke open the seventh seal, there was **silence** in heaven for about half an hour.'
Revelation 8:1 (the numbers of his birthdate)

Is God showing us who Elvis really is? (103–104)

Godfrey appeals to the writings of Nostradamus and Edgar Cayce, as well as to other Bible verses, to strengthen her claim that Elvis is the Lamb of God. Some of it reads like pure farce. Jesus' prediction that the Son of Man will come like lightning is taken as a reference to Elvis's lightning-bolt TCB symbol. Elvis wore a lionhead medallion, to symbolize that he was the Lion of Judah talked of in scripture. The Bible says that God calls his son 'out of Egypt.' Elvis got his start in Memphis, Tennessee, named after the ancient Egyptian city. Practically any verse of scripture seems, in Godfrey's interpretation, to point to Elvis Presley as the messiah. She also finds reference to Elvis in numerology, in close-up photographs of the Shroud of Turin and, not too surprisingly, in the constellation of Orion.

And what of Renee's hidden revelation, long-buried in the Michigan earth? It seems that in 1998, just before Godfrey's book went to press, the field was excavated by a construction crew. Search as she might, Renee was not able to find the document. This can only mean one thing, Godfrey assures us, the document has been found by a construction worker as predicted in 1958. The only step remaining is for it to be made public. Watch the tabloids! It is there that the proof of Elvis's divine nature will be fully revealed!

Elvis Religion Found!
Long Search by Would-Be Elvis Author Finally Complete
Details Inside

— Conclusion —

Okay, so maybe my actual conclusion doesn't match the catchy headline. Nevertheless, it does seem that in the writings of Godfrey we come closer than we have heretofore to a real, honest to goodness, non-ironic expression of Elvis religion. When Godfrey mixes the tabloid conspiracy theory of Brewer-Giorgio with a fundamentalist Christian interpretation of prophecy and a little touch of new age spirituality she arrives at something strikingly original. It is a theology of Elvis in which the many elements of the Elvis story come together in a syncretistic blend that could be a genuinely novel expression of religious faith. This is not to say, however, that Godfrey's book, or the existence of a group of like-minded individuals, constitutes the emergence of a new religious movement. Idiosyncratic theologies need some form of institutionalization in order to be cults. They need charismatic leaders, rituals, sacred objects, and sacred spaces. Namely, they need the kind of things we have looked for at Graceland and among Elvis impersonators, the kind of things we have looked for and failed to find. Esoteric religious doctrines, idiosyncratic theologies, and unique personal visions are simply that after all. They are esoteric, idiosyncratic, and personal. While Godfrey's religious vision of Elvis as the third, and final, incarnation of Adam/Jesus/Elvis is a remarkably creative vision, it remains more in the realm of quirky, individual beliefs than in the realm of cults and new religious movements.

This may indeed be where my late-night friend from the Memphis E.R. belongs. Perhaps I have been barking up the wrong tree by looking for an answer to the riddle of her devotion to Elvis among fans at Graceland or among Elvis impersonators. Perhaps popular movies, novels, and songs are the last place I should have looked for a glimpse of the secrets of her soul. Even Paul MacLeod's Graceland Too seems too public a place to find what I have been looking for. Perhaps I might find her hiding under cover of anonymity on an Elvis website. But the truth is that I probably will not find her in any of these places. Godfrey, no doubt, is an exception, someone who has dared to make her most private contemplations public even at the cost of publishing a book herself and, if her testimony is to be believed, losing her family along the way. My night-time emergency room acquaintance will probably live her life in anonymity, loving Elvis, believing in his grace and holiness, without setting pen to paper, without joining a church devoted to him, without opening her home to tourists. She is, in this sense, like Jesus on the road to Emmaus, who after sharing his faith with his fellow travelers disappeared from their midst.

9

Ironic Kingdom

Elvis and Religion in Popular (and Not so Popular) Culture

'Is Elvis dead?'

Those were the first words from her lips as she regained consciousness after a long and life threatening illness. After the operation things had appeared very uncertain. The doctor could not give any assurances that his mother would ever regain consciousness, that she would live to see another Christmas. She was elderly and frail, and what might have been surmountable for a younger woman was life threatening to her. So, when he saw her eyes flutter open and heard those words, he was truly shocked.

'Is Elvis dead?' she asked. If his mother had not been such an Elvis fan he probably would have asked her to repeat it, but she had been a fan for as long as he could remember so the question was not that off the wall, though at a time like this it wasn't exactly what one expected to hear.

I suppose that some people might have been bothered by the question. 'Is Elvis dead?' Why not, 'Son, it is so good to see you'? Or, if it must be a question, why not something like 'How is the family?' My friend, however, just shrugged it off. His mother, in coming back into the world of the conscious after a long sleep, had to determine not only who or where she was, but when she was. Who was easy, for we are who we are. Where wasn't hard either. Obviously she was in a hospital. But when, that's not something you can always tell just by looking around. You have to ask, 'What day is this?' or 'How long have I been unconscious?' My friend's mother went for a more important question first. It was a question like that a time traveler might ask when first stepping from the time machine. 'What era is this?', 'What period of time have I arrived in?', or in his mother's case, 'What part of my life is this? Where do we stand in the history of the twentieth century? Has man walked on the moon? Is Elvis dead?'

Without batting an eye, my friend gave it to her straight. 'Yes, mama, Elvis is dead.'

Well, call me crazy if you like. Say that this is another case of a supposed objective observer getting caught up in the story. But, I don't think my friend was right. Elvis dead? Not hardly.

— Poor Boys and Pilgrims —

All one has to do to see that Elvis is not dead is take a trip to Memphis, Tennessee, especially around the anniversaries of his birth or his death. Hang out in the nearby hotel bars, or at the Graceland Plaza shops. Listen to conversations. Introduce yourself. Or, failing that, pay close attention to you local newspaper. Sooner or later an Elvis impersonator contest is bound to come to a city near you. Drop in, plan to stay a few hours, long enough to get the feel of the event and the great sense of reverence the participants have for Elvis Presley. Without falling into the trap of comparing what happens at Graceland or on the Elvis impersonator circuit to a cult or a religion, we nevertheless have to admit that Elvis is extremely important in the lives of a lot of people. Maybe not as important for as many people as we might like to think, but for those who gather at Graceland for scavenger hunts, club meetings, auctions, contests, charity functions, and memorial services and for those who spend a small fortune to try to look and sound like Elvis, it is clear that Elvis plays a central role in their lives.

To wonder why this is the case is really to ask two very different questions. The first is a question about the psychological, sociological, and perhaps even pathological reasons that people would be so attracted to Elvis Presley. This is an extremely difficult question to answer, for there are probably as many reasons as there are Elvis fans, and I am not saying this just as an excuse to avoid the question. Different people find Elvis appealing for very different reasons. Some have come to associate Elvis with a more innocent time in American culture, that time after World War II and before Vietnam when it seemed possible that peace and prosperity would last forever. Some people are absolutely taken by his music. This is not to be shrugged off to quickly, either. For his music, when it was good, was nearly perfect and like nothing that had ever been heard before. Some probably are drawn to him by an overwhelming sexual attraction. Perhaps this attraction to Elvis was, for many, the first real erotic crush they ever had and one that has not been quick to go away. Some of them are drawn not so much to Elvis as to the community of Elvis fans themselves, which serves as an extended family and a network of friends. Perhaps dressing like Elvis gives some impersonators a sexual rush or livens up their sex life. Perhaps they dream of making it big and see Elvis as a way into show business. Maybe some of them, Graceland visitor or Elvis tribute artist, see in Elvis the signs of divinity or a way of salvation. There is no single answer to the question of why people are drawn to Elvis. This is only one question that has to be asked, however, in an attempt to understand why the memory of Elvis Presley lives on.

Elvis religion

The other question, of course, has to do with Elvis himself. Instead of asking what it is about fans that draw them to Elvis we must also ask what it is about Elvis that makes him such a draw. Though the answer to this question may be easier than the first, it is still pretty complex. What is it about Elvis that made him the sensation of a nation, that took him from a Mississippi shanty to the *Ed Sullivan Show*, that made teenage girls faint, and teenage boys change their hairstyle and dress? And what is it about Elvis that keeps his image vibrant and alive some thirty years after his messy, messy death? The answers are, of course, complex.

For one thing, Elvis was an incredible talent. His voice was enticing as was the style of music that he chose to record. Add to this his obvious good looks and his shocking dance steps and it is not hard to see why he was such a sensation. He was a vibrant, energizing, mesmerizing performer. This was true even when his image was broadcast in poor quality black-and-white pictures and when Ed Sullivan refused to show footage of him except from the waist up. Furthermore, despite the jokes, Elvis remained a good performer until near the end of his life. Oh, the last couple of years were difficult, when he was obviously overweight and under the influence of drugs, but from his Comeback Special to his many Las Vegas performances, Elvis put on quite a show.

It is also true that part of the attraction of Elvis is that, despite his fame, he remained strongly connected to his southern home and to his family. Though he owned a home in southern California, the fact that he maintained his primary residence in Memphis, Tennessee served to foster a bond between Elvis and the Memphis community that does not often occur with big-name celebrities. Call him a 'big fish is a small pond' in reference to his Memphis residence if you wish, but he was a big fish that was loved and adored by the other fish. While Bob Dylan has written that he moved to Woodstock to try and escape the fans who were constantly at his door and other celebrities simply avoid the problem by living in exclusive neighborhoods beyond the reach of the common fans, Elvis lived right there in the neighborhood, just around the block from his old high school, and fans were not only welcomed at his gate they were encouraged by the opportunity to talk to one of Elvis's relatives who sat in the guard house. Seeing as how Elvis was, for the most part, the only superstar in town, it is not too surprising that residents of the mid-south took him into their hearts.

This relationship with Elvis did not change after his death. Southerners always visit at the homes of the deceased, bringing food and sympathy. That is what people did for Elvis. They came to visit after his death and were so welcomed, especially when the house was open for public touring, that they just kept coming back. Graceland gave fans a place to gather and merchandise to collect and, over time, visiting there became one of those rituals of life, and I don't necessarily mean religious rituals either, I mean one of those rituals like family reunions or high-school home-comings where people go back year after year, time after time just to reminisce and see old friends. And all because of the person who was Elvis Presley, who according to the memories of his fans really did give Cadillacs away and love his mama, and appreciate his fans.

It is, no doubt, many of the same facts that drive the Elvis impersonator phenomenon. It is because Elvis was such a fantastic performer and because he was, at the same time, a lot like you and me that people have come to dress like and perform as Elvis Presley. Psycho-sexual explanations, ironic explanations, economic explanations, even religious explanations, must take account of this fact. For whatever reasons people impersonate Elvis they impersonate *Elvis* because he was both a superstar and an average guy all at the same time. No one wants to impersonate a talentless nobody. No one dares impersonate a god who is beyond their reach, no matter how many gifts and graces such a being may possess. But, an ordinary man with god-like talent? That I can at least try to do. Because Elvis was such a man, with great talent but of humble origins and humble pretensions, there is no way he could die. In Graceland and Vegas, in the hearts of fans and impersonators, Elvis lives!

— Outside, Underground, and Way Out —

It is not only in the fringe cultures of fan clubs and impersonator contests that Elvis has managed to live on after his death, however. He has also managed to stay alive in subcultures even more idiosyncratic than those associated with Graceland and Elvis Expo. He has managed to stay alive in the individual artistic visions of such people as Paul MacLeod, Howard Finster, and Joni Mabe. He lives on the internet in the form of anonymous tributes both sincere and ironic. He lives on in the tabloids, and in the individual lives of supermarket shoppers who take the tabloids home and devour every word. What makes these incarnations of Elvis Presley different from those of Graceland and tribute artists is their striking individuality. These artists and webmasters and theologians are not part of fan clubs or talent agencies. They are, for the most part, individuals who pursue their passion for Elvis outside such organizations. What makes these incarnations different from those seen in popular culture is that they exist on the fringes of that culture, instead of in the heart of it. What we find at the borders of our culture are esoteric and radically individualistic visions.

Because of the fact that these visions of Elvis come from outside, underground, and in some cases way out, they are,

of course, by definition odd and eccentric. They will probably always remain out of the mainstream. Like fans and
impersonators, they express incredible devotion to Elvis
Presley. For a multitude of reasons, however, not the least
of which is that their extreme devotion surpasses even that
of the most devoted fan club presidents, they are not a part
of this culture. It is not too surprising, therefore, to realize
that it is often among these eccentric individuals that we
find this devotion to Elvis accompanied by religious interpretations of his significance. While fan clubs and
impersonators are clearly devoted to the King, it has been
popular culture as it exists beyond the fan community that
has most clearly placed Elvis in a religious context. In these
movies, books, and novels, however, these religious proclamations are not tied directly to any personal devotion. The
Elvis fans have devotion. Filmmakers, novelists, and songwriters have the religious vision. These two elements,
personal devotion and religious interpretation, do show up
together, however, in the lives of the Elvis outsiders.

Though I do not want to over-generalize this point it is
nevertheless the case that it is often the people on the
fringes who put the two, devotion and religious doctrine,
together. I have in mind, of course, Howard Finster's cate-
gorization of Elvis as a saint, websites, both sincere and
ironic, devoted to Elvis churches, and Cinda Godfrey's brilliant blend of Christianity, spirituality, and Elvis
conspiracy theories. Here we see, more clearly than in the
world of Elvis fandom or the world of popular culture,
people devoted to their religious visions of Elvis. (I am not
overlooking those artists and webmasters who espouse
Elvis faith ironically, but see that as a special case of devotion to Elvis combined with a religious vision. More on this
a little later.)

What this means is that those interpreters who insist on
making the claim that Elvis devotion is a new religious
movement or some form of a cult will have to be a little

disappointed. It is unlikely that this kind of idiosyncratic, eccentric, and individual appropriation of Elvis Presley for religious meaning is now, or ever will become, the stuff of a genuine religious movement. It is interesting to see how Elvis fits into the religious worldviews of Howard Finster or Cinda Godfrey, but not likely that either worldview will grow to be accepted by a large number of people.

— At a Theater Near You —

My contention that Elvis religion is a phenomenon for the extreme margins of society and that the phenomena associated with Graceland and Elvis impersonators fail to qualify for this category does not mean that I fail to see any importance for Elvis Presley as a religious figure or icon, however. It only means that I do not think that religious appropriations of Elvis Presley are likely to spawn religious movements. Elvis, however, is, in more ways than I ever imagined when I started on this journey, an important religious image at the beginning of the twenty-first century. The religiousness of Elvis is played out in works of popular entertainment rather than at shrines, on pilgrimages, or in churches. This is fitting, I suppose, for that is where Elvis has always lived, on movie screens and on the radio. He has simply branched out now into literature, some of it a bit high brow for his own taste perhaps, but entertaining nevertheless. Elvis, we must not forget, was an entertainer. It is in the world of entertainment that he continues to live. In movies, books, and music he continues to entertain.

The roles he now plays, however, are decidedly different from those he played before his death. Had he lived and continued to make movies, this would probably still be the case. However, as I have already argued, it is in many ways because of his death that Elvis is cast in these new roles.

At their heart, and this theme even runs beyond popular culture to the world of outsider artists and internet churches, religious images of Elvis Presley are ironic images. This irony primarily takes one of two forms. In the first, the irony of the religious significance of Elvis is illustrated through a juxtaposition of Elvis's religious features with his tragic or ridiculous features. In the second, the irony takes the form of pretense and dissimulation. Elvis's religious nature is loudly proclaimed with tongue placed firmly in cheek.

Here is My Body, Bloated for You

The fact that Elvis is not really dead should be clear to anyone who has at all kept track of the world of popular movies, novels, and music. How could a dead man star in films? Yet there he is, larger than life on the big screen. There he is solving crimes in mystery novels. And listen, someone is singing about him on the radio! In the world of popular culture – film, fiction, and music – religious imagery is frequently evoked in reference to Elvis Presley. That religious evocation, however, is seldom straightforward, but often ambiguous and ironic. In the world of film Elvis appears as a vision of violence or, at best, as an ambiguous angel. In fiction, his messiah-ship is tempered by the fact of his humble origins and his tragic end. When he saves, often through his impersonators, he uses their flaws, their obesity, their all-too-humanness to save. In songs, the loudest and most clear proclamations of Elvis's religious meaning are usually given in jest.

It seems that, despite the religious attributions bestowed upon Elvis in popular culture, that culture is primarily realist at heart. For all that might be said about Elvis's great talent or looks, about his character or virtues, these films and books and songs are all produced after his death. We have all seen the photographs taken of him shortly before his death, how he had gained weight and looked pale and fat. We all know how his last performances made it clear that his talent was being eaten away by demons and drugs. We all know that he died in his bathroom. After August 17, 1977, how can anyone help but be a realist? How can anyone ignore the fact that even our best, our very best, can be cut down and lost in ways that remain beyond our control?

In the American psyche the death of Elvis may not be of the same importance as the assassinations of the Kennedy brothers, or of Dr. Martin Luther King. It is clearly not as profound and tragic as the destruction of the World Trade Center. Nevertheless, more than Elvis was lost on that day, at least in part because we could see that he had done this to himself. He was not assassinated, not murdered, not the victim of some tragic crime. He simply ate and doped himself to death. And that, you see, is the way that most of us will die, in stupid ways, from smoking too much, or drinking too much, or eating too much, or driving too fast, or having a stroke on the toilet. Elvis's death was not the death of a political figure; he did not die as a symbol of anything. He died like the rest of us, too early and without any rhyme or reason.

I remember reaching my cousin Theresa's house on that hot, August afternoon of Elvis's death and finding her in tears. She had ripped all of her Elvis posters off the wall and wadded them up beyond recognition. She screamed. She swore, using language that I would never have said within earshot of my parents. Elvis was dead. The posters that I thought marked her transition from childhood to adulthood, the posters that I would never have been able to put up on my wall because I was too young, all came down. And that, that was real adulthood. It meant no posters, no idols, and no fantasies. Upon hearing the news of Elvis's death I had immediately taken off in a run to Theresa's house because she was the biggest Elvis fan I knew. She would be able tell me what it meant. This is what it meant. I see this now in ways that I never did then.

'Yes, mama, Theresa, Virginia, Elvis is dead.'

But he is not. He is still there, in movies, books and songs. In all of those instances, however, he is there *and* dead, if not for the other characters in the stories, then for us. We can't avoid it. Our sons and daughters and mothers and fathers and cousins are always honest with us. 'Is Elvis dead?' 'Yes.' Stories of Elvis's postmortem, then, are bound to be stories of violence and ambiguity. They are bound to be stories that show us, no matter how much we want to believe in gods and fairy tales, that we are only human. Even Elvis was only human. We must either see that because we are all flawed, there can be no real gods or heroes, or that if we are going to have gods and heroes we must take them as they are.

This is why, I suppose, the Elvis of Val Kilmer, Kevin Costner, Bruce Campbell, Harvey Keitel, Nicolas Cage, and all the others are so flawed, so human, so real. This is why novels about Elvis focus on his addiction or the limits of his impoverished upbringing. The gods now walk among us. Elvis is dead and the fact that he lives on in popular culture incarnations is not at odds with this, indeed it is because of this. If Elvis had not died, if he had not died in the way he did, would there be movies about him still today, would he figure in novels and pop songs? Of course not. He lives, because he died. He shows us the violent visions, the ambiguity of angels, the fact that even our best messiahs come from Memphis and wear tacky jumpsuits.

Ironic Kingdom, or What's So Funny About Saint Elvis?

All of this taken alone, however, neglects another important aspect of the way Elvis appears to us in popular culture. It is not only the case that his flaws, his huge appetites, and his sad decline and death are juxtaposed with his god-like qualities in a way that reminds us of the limits of human life and human potential. It is also the case, thankfully, that the opposite is true. Elvis's flaws, his huge appetites, and his sad decline and death are embraced and divinized. It is not always that we must say Elvis was a transcendent figure despite his humanity. We may also say, thankfully, that Elvis was a transcendent figure because of his humanity. Indeed, I suppose, this is how Elvis really saves.

Look, let's all admit, including all of you later-years impersonators out there, Elvis started out on fire but he did not end up that way. When he came on the scene the world had never seen anything like him. He was perfection in his sound and his looks, and many must have imagined in his touch and his feel as well. This did not last, however. He made a lot of bad movies. Sure, some of them were okay, but a lot of them were bad. There was the Comeback Special, of course, Elvis in black leather looking just as good as ever, maybe even better. But then things started to go downhill. Tragically, he died before he could have another comeback. The indelible image of Elvis Presley that we are left with is of a pasty-faced, pudgy, middle-aged guy in a ridiculous white jumpsuit, singing 'Poke Salad Annie' and 'In the Ghetto'. Add to this all of the redneck, white-trash elements of his personality that his closest friends could not seem to tell us enough about and you really start to see how Elvis borders on being nothing but a great, big joke. (Some of these are not even specific to Elvis; they are just bits of his lower-class, white, southern culture that were never understood outside the south. He loved peanut-butter-and-banana sandwiches. Big deal! So do I. Sometimes we rednecks even put mayonnaise on them instead of peanut butter. The mayonnaise makes them a little lighter for summertime dining. He said 'thank you, thank you very much.' Well that's how our mamas raised us to talk. We southerners thank everybody for everything, thank you.)

Now, if somebody says this big, fat, 'bubba' is the messiah, the savior, the second coming of Jesus Christ, they've got to be kidding, right? Of course they've got to be kidding. The Presleyterian Church of Elvis, the Divine, the Twenty-Four Hour Church of Elvis, Joni Mabe's Elvis toenail and wart icons, Mojo Nixon singing 'Elvis is Everywhere'; it's all a joke. It is a joke at the expense of big ol' fat latter-day Elvis, a joke at the expense of Elvis fans and impersonators, a joke at the expense of southerners, and a joke at the expense of people everywhere with bad taste. And sometimes, as a man who falls into at least two of the categories, the joke can hurt.

But 'no pain, no gain,' they say, and this is no different, because this is a joke that saves as well as hurts. For what is in one sense a joke at the expense of such things is also, in another sense, a celebration of them. Elvis is the King, not despite the peanut-butter-and-banana sandwiches but because of them. He is the King, not despite the fact that he once ripped his pants on stage because he had gained a little too much weight, but because he ripped his pants on stage. He is just the kind of god we need these days. He is overweight, spends too much money on prescription drugs, and dresses more than a few years behind the fashion of the day. He is also just the kind of god we need these days because he cannot be taken too seriously. In this age of religious fundamentalism, of people who take their religion so seriously that they are more than willing to kill anyone who disagrees with them, it sure is refreshing to contemplate Saint Elvis, not the best god in the world, not the most perfect, not the most fashionable nor the most fit, but more than a little funny. Is Elvis a joke? No way. But there sure are a lot of funny jokes about Elvis.

Postscript

Pass the Elvis-Themed Lunchbox and Thermos Salt-and-Pepper Shaker Set, Please

What would I do differently if I could live that night in the emergency room over again? Would I stay around the waiting room until I made sure that she and her mother were taken care of? After all, she had confessed that she was alone in Memphis, without family or loved ones. Maybe I could buy her a cup of coffee, my way of 'lighting a candle for Elvis.' I know that given the chance I would ask her more about Elvis. Why was she so devoted to him? What did he mean to her? Had she ever seen him perform in concert or met him in person? Did she buy her Elvis jewelry at Graceland Plaza or did she make it herself? Did her mother feel the same way about Elvis that she did? Does she like Elvis impersonators or Elvis movies? Had she ever visited Graceland Too?

What would I do if I could see her again today, that messenger of Elvis from so long ago, my own ambiguous angel? I would probably invite her over to my house for dinner. I would slice up some bananas and open up a jar of peanut butter. My wife would make fried chicken and mashed potatoes. We would talk about Elvis, the King, Big E until the kids fell asleep on the floor, until the blue moon turned to gold, until Elvis had left the building.

Bibliography

Abani, Chris. (2004). *Graceland* (New York, Farrar, Straus, and Giroux)

Brewer-Giorgio, Gail. (1979). *Orion: The Living Superstar of Song* (New York, Pocket Books)

—— (1988). *Is Elvis Alive?* (New York, Tudor)

—— (1990). *The Elvis Files: Was his Death Faked?* (New York, Shapolsky)

Chadwick, Vernon (ed). (1997). *In Search of Elvis: Music, Race, Art, Religion* (Boulder, CO, Westview Press)

Doss, Erika. (1999). *Elvis Culture: Fans, Faith, and Image* (Lawrence, KA, University Press of Kansas)

Duff, Gerald. (1995). *That's Alright Mama.* (Dallas, Baskerville)

Eicher, Peter. (1993). *The Elvis Sightings* (New York, Avon Books)

Giorgio, Gail. (1999). *Elvis Undercover: Is He Alive and Coming Back?* (Austin, TX, Bright Books)

Godfrey, Cinda. (1999). *The Elvis–Jesus Mystery: The Shocking Scriptural and Scientific Evidence that Elvis Presley Could Be the Messiah Anticipated throughout History* (New Philadelphia, OH, Revelation Publishing)

Gould, Jay. (1999). *Elvis 2000: The King Returns* (London, Glitterbooks)

Gregory, Neal and Janice. (1980). *When Elvis Died* (New York, Pharos Books)

Harrison, Ted. (1992). *Elvis People: The Cult of the King* (London, Fount)

Henderson, William McCranor. (1984). *Stark Raving Elvis* (New York, Berkeley)

—— (1997). *I, Elvis: Confessions of a Counterfeit King* (New York, Boulevard Books)

Hope, Christopher. (1997). *Me, the Moon, and Elvis Presley* (London, Macmillan)

Elvis religion

Jaffe, Paul. (1999). *Clothed in Light: Elvis' Soul Journey* (Grass Valley, CA, Elvis Presley Online)

Kluge, P. F. (1996). *Biggest Elvis* (New York, Penguin Books)

Laughlin, Bob. (2000). *The Gospel of Elvis* (New York, Dim Raft)

Lowy, Jonathan. (2001). *Elvis and Nixon* (New York, Crown)

Marcus, Greil. (1991). *Dead Elvis: A Chronicle of a Cultural Obsession* (New York, Doubleday)

Marg, Susan. (2004). *Las Vegas Weddings. A Brief History, Celebrity Gossip, Everything Elvis and the Complete Chapel Guide* (New York: Perennial)

Marino, Rick. (2000). *Be Elvis! A Guide to Impersonating the King* (Naperville, IL, Sourcebooks)

Paul, David and Geoffrey A. Todd. (2000). *Templars of the Christian Brotherhood* (Bloomington, IN, 1st Books)

Plasketes, George. (1997). *Images of Elvis Presley in American Culture: 1977–1997* (New York, Harrington Park Press)

Rodman, Gilbert B. (1996). *Elvis after Elvis: The Posthumous Career of a Living Legend* (London, Routledge)

Rubinowski, Leslie. (1997). *Impersonating Elvis* (Boston, Faber and Faber)

Sinclair, Carl R. (1996). *Elvis A. Eagle: A Magical Adventure* (New York, Scribe Press)

Strausbaugh, John. (1995). *E: Reflections of the Birth of the Elvis Faith* (New York, Blast Books)

Thomas-Williams, Pamela. (2003). *Elvis Lives: The Business of Being Elvis* (Lacrosse, WI, Books by Pamela)

Werner, Steve. (2000). *Elvis and the Apocalypse* (Philadelphia, Xlibris)

Wright, Daniel. (1996). *Dear Elvis: Graffiti from Graceland* (Memphis, Mustang Publishing)

Yenne, Bill. (1999). *The Field Guide to Elvis Shrines* (San Francisco, Last Gasp)

Index